DRAUGHTPROOFING
AND **INSULATION**
——— A PRACTICAL GUIDE ———

DRAUGHTPROOFING
AND INSULATION
A PRACTICAL GUIDE

TONY COWLING

THE CROWOOD PRESS

First published in 2023 by
The Crowood Press Ltd
Ramsbury, Marlborough
Wiltshire SN8 2HR

enquiries@crowood.com

www.crowood.com

British Library Cataloguing-in-Publication Data
A catalogue record for this book is available from the British Library.

ISBN 978 0 7198 4263 4

The ability to solve problems is one of the greatest things that our education system delivers and to be capable of doing this well is a key to succeeding in any walk of life.

Disclaimer
The author and publisher do not accept responsibility or liability in any manner whatsoever for any omissions, nor for any loss, damage, injury, or adverse outcome of any kind incurred as a result of the use of the information contained in this book or reliance upon it. Readers are advised to seek professional advice relating to their particular property project and circumstances before embarking on any building, draughtproofing project or related work.

Typeset and designed by D & N Publishing, Baydon, Wiltshire
Cover design by Nick May/www.bluegecko22.com
Printed and bound in India by Parksons Graphics Pvt. Ltd.

Contents

Heat loss is a problem that can be found in most homes. It not only adds to household bills but in the most severe cases can adversely affect quality of life. The purpose of this book is to help you to cut down the amount of energy you use, while hopefully improving your quality of life by reducing your bills and giving you a better environment in which to live.

The author of this book is the founder of the DraughtBusters scheme that started in Reading in December 2012. Transition Town Reading (TTR) was awarded a grant by Reading Borough Council to pay for materials for draughtproofing the homes of some of the most disadvantaged people in the borough. The project commenced in January 2013 using volunteers from both TTR and the Rotary Club of Reading. The scheme was initially limited to those who were living in poor conditions and in fuel poverty, especially if they were families with young children and on benefits or were very elderly. It also included those living in cold, draughty conditions who were under debt management.

What we found when visiting these homes was that by draughtproofing we could save these vulnerable households large amounts of money; in some cases, just a few simple measures made a huge difference. Keeping the cold and draughts out and stopping up all the unwanted sources of ventilation and heat loss from our dwellings are far and away the most cost-effective things to do in terms of saving money and should be the first point of call when trying to save energy.

Based on our experiences over the years, the aim of this book is twofold. Firstly, we will help you identify where the draughts are coming into the home. Secondly, we will give you practical pointers for eliminating draughts in the identified areas. The

What Does it Cost?

The lowest amount that DraughtBusters spent on a property was £1.50. We only needed caulk to save £40 p/a through reduced heat losses. If that particular household were to take our advice about heating control, a further £120 saving p/a would be easy to achieve. On average, each client cost just under £25 in the early years and annual savings in 2012 were estimated to be in the order of £100. As already mentioned, it is always easy to make the first lot of savings and further savings

become increasingly more difficult. The biggest saving was £600 p/a for a cost of £30. The returns on draughtproofing are always good but the return on £1.50 looks more like the interest on a payday loan than the return on draughtproofing a home. In all cases, the savings in the first year have been greater than the cost of materials.

Current costs are still £25 on average per home but the savings have risen dramatically after the energy price hikes, to 15 per cent of the heating bill – which equates to £300–£400 on average as at December 2022.

ultimate goal is to reach something called minimum energy use. This will be different for every house, and it is debatable whether it actually exists. It is nearly always possible to reduce energy consumption, but it becomes more and more difficult after you have done all the easy things. The aim of this practical guide is to get you as close to minimum energy use as possible.

Most of the suggestions are things that you can do yourself if you are a reasonably proficient DIYer. Some are very simple and basic craft skills will get you through them. The book also includes measures that you might want to get a builder or home energy specialist to do, perhaps alongside other planned work, for instance when you upgrade your heating system, refurbish your kitchen or bathroom, or build an extension. You should budget for this and plan to do it at the same time as other works. This will be the most economical point at which to carry out additional measures – not just air sealing, but insulation too.

Chapter One

Locating the Problem

Draughtproofing is by far the most economical thing you can do in terms of saving energy in your home. It is a relatively quick and easy way to reduce heat loss and cut heating bills. In a typical house, draughts can account for 10 per cent of total heat loss, and much more if there is an unused fireplace (yougen.co.uk/2009/04/22/draughts-can-be-cured/). Draughtproofing costs are low and the benefits were huge even before the energy price hike. In the early 2010s we calculated that draughtproofing would save about £120 a year on heating bills; we now think it probably saves more like £250 a year in 2022. You can save up to 15 per cent of your heating bill by stopping draughts. Every house is different, but it is usually easy to do things to save 10 percent; the next 5 per cent is more difficult to realise.

This of course only applies if you can afford to run your heating as previously. A further energy price hike of 77 per cent is predicted, and if that happens then the savings will increase to as much as £400. Please note that DraughtBusters' costs will be a bit lower than your costs because we buy very carefully in bulk and avoid certain popular suppliers. Even so, you can see that it is going to be money well spent.

How to Find Draughts in Your Home

The book will go into greater detail in later chapters, but here are some initial pointers for you. By following these you will already have made a very good start on the task.

First Glance

When I visit a property, before I knock on the front door, I briefly check the outside of the building, looking for air vents, holes or gaps that could let in draughts. As I walk in through the front door, I look for things that could be draughty or cause draughts. I note the presence or absence of draught strips on the front door frame, letterplate seals, weather bar, locks and keyholes. Moving further in, I cast an eye towards any holes around radiator pipes, gaps in floorboards and/or under skirtings.

Downstairs

Front door Letterbox – is yours draughty?

Living rooms Are there any old air vents that are no longer needed? Are there gaps under skirtings or around heating pipes? Check for draughts under window boards and around windows. Are the window casements draught-free, do the windows shut properly and do trickle ventilators close? If there is a chimney, is it used sometimes or never? If the chimney is not used at all, then fit a chimney balloon or shove an old pillow in a black sack up it. If ventilated, close the vent.

Kitchen Are there any holes around pipes leading to outside? Are there redundant ventilation grilles, draughty windows or a draughty back door? Does the fan or cooker hood have a back draught flap or shutter?

Figs 1.1 and 1.2 Draughts can come in under sills, in this case patio door sills with big draughts coming from the cavity. The underside of the patio door sill had been sealed but many aren't.

Upstairs

Loft I check the loft trap for draughtproofing strips and note whether it is insulated or not. In the loft I look for daylight. It is acceptable to see daylight when looking down through ventilation slots and between tiles or slates, but not upwards through roof coverings. I check the insulation, how thick it is, and whether there are gaps or bits missing. Are the cistern(s) and pipework, including the overflow pipe, insulated? Is there a draughty gap around where the soil pipe or other pipes go down into the house?

Airing cupboards Are there any gaps around pipes, or old pipe holes that have not been filled or covered, going up into the loft?

Bathroom Is there a fan? Can the window be left open in a secure ventilating position to provide background ventilation when needed?

Bedrooms Are there any gaps under window boards or around the window frames? Are the window sashes draughtproof and do the hinges, friction stays and handles all work? Are there disused air vents? Are there any gaps under skirtings? These can be draughty even upstairs!

Airtightness and Draughts

Older houses, and even a lot of new ones, can still be very draughty and consequently expensive to run as they waste a lot of heated air, losing it through fans and draughts. Draughts occur where there are unwanted gaps in the construction of your home, and where openings, holes, slits or cracks are left unsealed. Draughts are different from ventilation because draughts are uncontrolled and uncontrollable. We like controllable ventilation. New homes are required to meet minimum airtightness standards (Part L of the Building Regulations – Conservation of Fuel and Power). However, the standard is poor and often not met.

Some homes go further and aim to meet the UK or International Passivhaus standard (passivhaus. org.uk). These will be very airtight and, as part of the design, they will have a ventilation system and will recover energy from the exhaust airstream; this air will be warm, and a mechanical ventilation and heat recovery system will operate. These recover heat from the outgoing air stream and deliver it back into the home with the new fresh air that comes in from outside.

The Importance of Ventilation

Before you rush off to seal your home, it is worth stressing that all homes need to be ventilated. Controlled ventilation helps ensure that the air in your home stays fresh and that humidity doesn't rise to a level where it becomes a problem. There are also some parts of your home where ventilation is important to the health of the building, for example in the void under a suspended timber ground floor and in your loft. We'll flag these sorts of considerations wherever they come up.

Protecting Against Damp and Condensation

One of the arguments often given for not bothering to draughtproof is that doing so increases the likelihood of damp and condensation. There is some truth in this, but it is a good example of confusing draughts and controlled ventilation. *See* Chapter 3 for more on the typical causes of damp and condensation in buildings and some simple measures you can take to help reduce the levels of condensation in your home.

Chapter Two

Air Sealing

Air sealing is a more thorough and detailed process than draughtproofing and looks at all the tiny gaps and cracks in a building with the aim of making the building airtight. I can already hear you saying, 'I like the draughts and I need ventilation'. Yes, you are right, you do need ventilation, but you don't need or want draughts. These are uncontrollable and lose you heat, causing higher than necessary energy use and costing you money. Ventilation must be controllable.

Fig 2.2 Opening windows is the best way to ventilate rooms.

Fig 2.1 Opening windows works very well when ventilation is needed.

Air sealing is the process by which all gaps, cracks, holes and ducts in a wall, floor or ceiling through which draughts may be able to enter are sealed. This is easiest to do during construction; however, sadly, for most of us this will not have been done then and so will have to be carried out retrospectively.

Brick-Built Houses

It is not at all easy to air seal your home. You have first to decide where your air barrier is. It can be the paint, the plaster finish or the plaster itself; it can be the membrane that lies behind the linings, or it may be the sheathing or a membrane on the outside of a timber frame. It can't be the blockwork or brickwork because these normally have holes in them; indeed, the blocks themselves may even be porous to air infiltration.

If you draw a cross-section through your home then it should be possible to put a pencil on the air barrier and to follow it right through the section, up the wall and across a window, over the lintel to the top of the wall; then across the ceiling, down the other wall and through the floor void to the ground floor wall; then across the floor, up through your door threshold, door and door head, then up the other wall and finally again through the first-floor void. If you can do this without taking your pencil off the paper then you've just successfully air sealed your home – at least in theory.

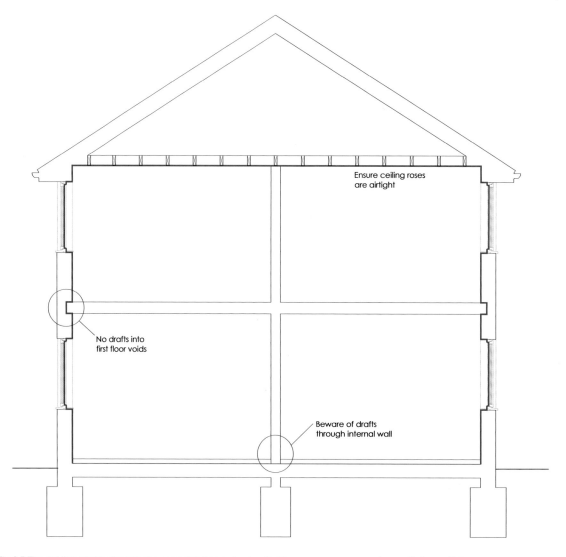

Ensure ceiling roses are airtight

No drafts into first floor voids

Beware of drafts through internal wall

Fig 2.3 The red line on this diagram shows an airtightness barrier. Problems can occur everywhere with these. Make no assumptions: everything is prone to air leakage, closed trickle ventilators can be draughty, and there can be cracks in plaster or gaps under sills. The theory is easy but in practice it is nearly impossible to achieve a completely airtight barrier.

Converting theory into reality isn't nearly so easy. By far the most difficult area to deal with is the first-floor void, and this will be covered in greater detail in Chapter 13. However, it is relatively easy if you choose paint or finishing plaster as your airtight layer because you can see it, and if there are cracks you can fill them. Having done that, the next problem is joining your walls to windows, pipes, ducts, door thresholds, skirtings and floors. If you have suspended wooden floors, these will be the second-biggest problem. There can be gaps between the floorboards and there will certainly be gaps and cracks all around the edge of every floor.

These are difficult to seal. My preferred method is to take all the floorboards up, insulate the floor and add a combined air barrier and vapour barrier on top of the joists. Then replace the floorboards and trap the air barrier behind the skirtings. If you're diligent enough to do that, you can then go on to consider what happens where a door lining touches the floorboard, as there is now a gap along the edge of the floorboard that the lining is sitting on. The gap will allow air from under the floor to come up behind the door lining and then out, for example, above the top architrave, through the latch hole, or from behind any of the architraves.

These problems aren't easy to solve. However, it is possible and you don't have to do it all at once. Air sealing is an advanced process, often only undertaken by the most dedicated of homeowners.

Timber-Framed Buildings

We have so far only considered traditionally constructed homes made of bricks and blocks with wooden floors. If you have concrete planks or beam and block floors in that type of house, then you still need to consider air sealing. There are some pointers in Chapter 9 about how to do this.

Timber-framed homes have a different set of problems. At this point it is worth considering what happens in Canada, where most of the homes are timber-framed. Canadians build their homes in much the same way as we do: frame up first, roof on, then services are added and then insulation works are carried out. The walls are usually filled with fibreglass or rockwool quilt and the lofts are blown completely full of fibreglass fibres.

The next thing that happens in Canada is that a vapour barrier is applied to the walls and ceilings. They are completely obsessive about how well this is applied, because even a tiny pinhole in the vapour barrier can cause a build-up of moisture in the frame itself, and if this happens the moisture turns to ice in winter and then starts to form an iceberg inside the wall, which will continue to grow until it forces off either the cladding or the plasterboard lining! This vapour barrier is then inspected and, if necessary, any rectifications are carried out before the plasterboarding is done. During the process of plasterboarding, any damages are repaired. The airtightness test results on such houses are so much better than ours that we simply don't believe them.

For building regulations, our airtightness tests used to allow ten air changes an hour at a pressure differential of 50 pascals, although five is now a more common target. When a building is tested, a powerful calibrated fan is fitted into one of the openings and used to pressurise it to 50 Pa. The volume of air that the fan needs to push into the building is then calculated in terms of the volume of that building and the result is quoted as a number of air changes per hour. We call this the air leakage rate; it can also be measured in cubic metres of air needed per hour per square metre of the envelope. In Canada it is common to achieve less than 0.1 air changes per hour! Homes there are very airtight, and ours are like colanders in comparison.

If you have a timber-framed house, you need to seal all cracks and gaps, sorting out ducts and pipe boxings, sealing where they pass through the airtightness layer, and sealing soil pipe boxes top and bottom. Then check under window boards, around the loft trap, including the architraves, and around all window and door frames between the frame and the wall. You must also check underneath all thresholds and sills on patio doors. We find a lot of draughts under these, and they often need sealing both internally and externally.

General Sealing

Looking for draughts is simple to start with but gets progressively more difficult. The best plan is to have a good look at all your walls, floors and ceilings, trying to inspect everywhere. Any cracks or gaps that look a little dark will almost certainly be letting in draughts, as the dark staining is due to dust coming in with the draughts. These can be in the corners, against windows, between window sills and windows, under window sills, between a sash and the frame, under a door frame or around pipes. Look in the backs and tops of cupboards and at the soil pipe where it goes through the loft or out through the wall.

It is very difficult to inspect inside a soil pipe box; sometimes we resort to drilling a small hole and foam filling at ground-floor, first-floor and roof level, and if a pipe exits through the cavity then filling at that point. Great care is needed, and we usually advise the use of fixing foam rather than expanding foam as there can be serious problems with overfilling using expanding foam; it can stress or even move the boxing.

Services such as gas, water, electricity and telecoms often enter the house through ducts or drilled holes, and these all need sealing. The water service pipe may be coming in through a 100mm duct and this can be draughty. Usually, we push rolled-up polythene down the duct first and then fill over the top with foam. Gas pipes should be sealed to their ducts on the inside only, **not** both inside and outside; the duct itself should be sealed to the wall both inside and outside.

Avoid downlighters at all costs. If you have downlighters, a smoke hood or some secondary boxing in should be carried out, then insulation. Proprietary metal covers can also be fitted.

Figs 2.4 and 2.5 Soil vent pipes going through ceilings. Draughts can enter around these pipes. Note that the insulation, which was only 100mm thick, was pulled back for these photographs.

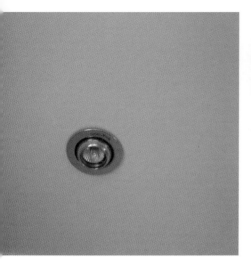

Fig 2.6 Downlighter.

Fig 2.7 A downlighter viewed from above.

Fig 2.8 A more modern downlighter with integral enclosure. This will still be letting in some draughts even when covered by the insulation, which has been lifted up for the photograph.

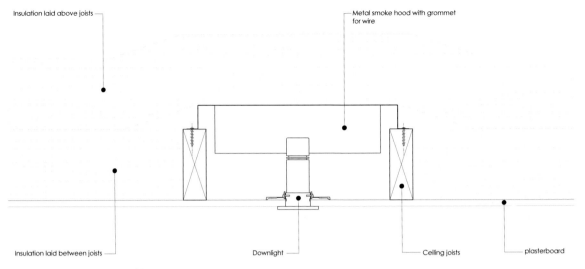

Insulation laid above joists

Metal smoke hood with grommet for wire

Insulation laid between joists

Downlight

Ceiling joists

plasterboard

Fig 2.9 Metal cover for a downlighter.

Fig 2.10 A typical crack under a window board that will be letting in draughts.

Fig 2.12 A window board crack sealed with decorator's caulk.

Fig 2.11 A window board crack above a radiator. We could see daylight through this particular crack. We caulked it from the inside and asked the client to get the outside sealed too.

Chapter Three

Ventilation, Draughts and Condensation

There are conflicts between ventilation, draughts and preventing condensation. We see that good ventilation is crucially important. The adage 'build tight, ventilate right' is a very good one and we could extend it to say, 'live airtight, ventilate right'. It is especially important to ventilate underfloor voids and most lofts, roofs and chimneys (*see* Chapter 7).

We often come across people who say they have no condensation in their homes, and we suspect they may be living in very draughty buildings. Others think that draughts are good because they get rid of condensation.

A more constructive way to look at it, however, is that draughts are bad because they take away a lot of heat from the home, and that it is far better not to have any draughts and to open windows or switch on fans when ventilation is needed. The reason for this is very simple: you don't need to ventilate all the time. We certainly don't need to run a bathroom fan or have a window open all day; in fact, we like them to be closed most of the time, especially in winter. They should be opened for a short period every morning in bedrooms and the rest of the home should be ventilated as and when required.

So how should we get rid of condensation? We advocate opening bathroom or shower room windows or running a fan for a short period of time after the room has been used for bathing or showering. Additionally, we suggest squeegeeing or wiping tiled surfaces, shower doors, screens, and so on after use. If carried out immediately, this simple action removes most of the water that has condensed on those surfaces, meaning that less ventilation time is required to dry the surfaces and a lot less heat is lost.

Draughts from Fans

Extractor Fans

Extractor fans are now a statutory requirement and must be fitted in all new bathrooms, utility rooms and kitchens. Herein lies a huge problem. Extractor fans do exactly what they say they do: they extract air from the home, dumping it outside. The drawback is that they take out heated air and throw it away. In a completely airtight building, an extractor fan would extract a small amount of air from the building, depressurising it slightly, and then do nothing except make a noise. There is something illogical going on when we combine the idea of airtightness with an extractor fan. Sadly, in the real world this is never a problem because our buildings are so leaky that air is sucked in through all the little gaps and cracks that we at DraughtBusters strive to seal up.

My own house was designed to be very airtight and is probably one of the most airtight masonry homes of its age in the country. I installed a mechanical heat recovery ventilation system (MVHR). I have a big box with two fans in it in my plant room. Inside it there is a heat exchanger that strips the heat out of the outgoing air stream and transfers it to the incoming fresh air stream. New fresh air flows into all my living rooms and bedrooms through outlets in the ceilings of each of those rooms and stale, used air is extracted from bathrooms, cloakrooms, utility room, hallway, plant room and kitchen. I don't have a heating system and can't afford to throw away any heat; by using an MVHR, the air in my house is always lovely and fresh and we don't need to open

Figs 3.1–3.6 Window on vent, partly open, both sides open, both sides open fully and shown from outside.

windows – although my wife still loves opening windows in the morning!

Extractor fans in the homes of those in energy poverty never get switched on and sometimes they are blocked up deliberately by tenants or homeowners. This is bad for both the building and the occupants. As soon as there is mould around, there are health hazards, which can be very serious, and the fabric of the building starts to decay too.

One of the main reasons that people block up extractor fans is because they are draughty. We often advise our clients to keep the bathroom or shower room door shut after use until everything has dried out. We even advocate opening a window very slightly in bathrooms and shower rooms and keeping the door shut to try to prevent damp, mould and condensation. This strategy does work, but it needs help: a diligent homeowner who is prepared to squeegee and wipe surfaces after showering or bathing and then hang the cloth or towel outside and not on the radiator will have fewer problems and less often than one who doesn't.

Extractor fans are available that have shutters on them that open and close depending on whether the fan is on or off; these are considerably more expensive than the fans that are usually fitted, which are the cheapest ones available from the supplier.

Cooker Hoods

I was recently helping a friend to seal some stains on their kitchen ceiling. We used gloss paint, which was quite smelly, so I switched on their cooker hood to try to help evacuate the fumes from the paint more quickly. The cooker hood didn't like it, however, and soon started flashing an error code. I later discovered that they had put a big ball of polythene in carrier bags inside the cooker hood between the filters and the fan, as it made the kitchen cold whether it was switched on or not, particularly if it was windy outside or in winter. Not surprisingly, when I then tried to use it, the fan motor got a bit too warm and

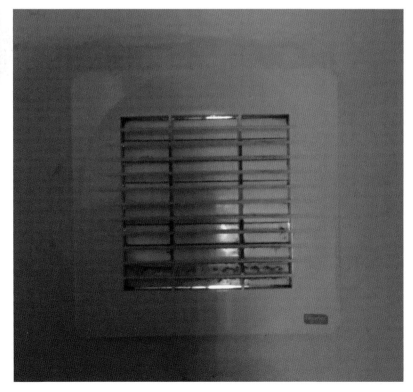

Fig 3.7 Extractor fan with daylight visible.

Fig 3.8 Extractor fan that needs to be cleaned.

switched itself off! Thankfully it worked again once the fan motor had cooled down, and I returned later to do the sealing.

So, what can be done about cooker hoods? They can have positive shutters so that they are closed when switched off; it would be sensible if the regulations required this. When it's very cold, you can push a big ball of polythene into the outlet pipe to stop draughts – just don't forget it's there when you need to use the hood! Alternatively, find an automated choke, throttle or electrically operated shutter for the outlet duct or terminal.

Bathroom and Utility Room Fans

These fans sit in a 100mm- or 150mm-diameter hole in the wall or ceiling of the room in question. That hole, even with a fan in it, causes draughts. This should not be the case, so ideally the requirements would be changed so that all extractor fans have positive close shutters on them, not the ones that flap and blow around in the wind and still let air out any time the wind gusts strongly enough. They need to be able to shut off the air flow, either by closing the pipe with an iris shutter or with an electrically operated choke. Sometimes we can see daylight through extractor fans, which means that they will be draughty.

Airtightness

Airtightness is a measure of how much air leaks into or out of a building. So that results can be easily compared, this is done at a pressure difference of 50 pascals (Pa). To measure airtightness, we install a fan into the building that can either pressurise or depressurise the building, and then measure the volume of air that is needed to maintain that pressure. The results are expressed as either air changes per hour at 50 Pa, or as cubic metres per hour per square metre of the envelope area. In the UK, the results usually fall in the range between ten and one. It is very difficult to find houses with results at the lower end of this range. I worked very hard on my own house, which is of masonry construction but wet plastered, and the result was just less than one. In Canada results commonly range from 0.3 to below 0.1. For new houses in the UK tested using this process, we usually now get results in the range of three to five or above.

Airtightness sealing is the process of finding and sealing up all the little gaps and cracks in the envelope, and is normally done during the construction process. It is very difficult to do it once the building is finished because some of the gaps are impossible to get at, for instance between the floor and the ceiling, in a pipe box or behind the plasterboard linings.

Trying to heat a leaky building is difficult and wasteful of energy.

Figs 3.13 and 3.14 show the blower door test being carried out on my house. The engineer told me he frequently can't pressurise new houses to 50 Pa and was surprised when I guaranteed that he would be able to get mine there. He then had problems turning the fan speed down very low and had to fit all his flow restrictor discs to be able to measure the volume of air my house used to keep it at 50 Pa. The process of testing, as mentioned above, is carried out by both pressurising and depressurising the building. Fitting restrictor discs reduces the volume of air that the fan can shift and is a very good indication of airtightness.

Fig 3.13 Airtightness testing using a blower door.

Fig 3.14 Blower door seen from inside the house.

Condensation

Condensation has many causes: lack of ventilation, missing insulation, very cold indoor surfaces, high humidity, drying washing indoors, cooking (particularly boiling), showering and bathing, and even breathing, as well as any other activity that adds moisture to the air inside a home.

The area of damp mould and condensation shown in Fig 3.15 was caused by a lack of ventilation. A chest of drawers had been pushed into the corner of the room. It was one of those that have a plinth and chipboard sides that come right down to the floor, so there was no air flow underneath it, and the gaps between the sides and the walls were quite small. This restricted the amount of warm air from the room that could flow around behind this piece of furniture. As you can see, mould took a fairly good hold here. There is always a colder patch in the corners of rooms; the concrete floor and a three-dimensional corner effect generally make the bottom corner the coldest place.

Mould frequently grows on the sealant up the corner join between the windows in the corner of a bay, where there is likely to be an uninsulated metal post. In Fig 3.17, note the small pool of water at the bottom. These problems are difficult to solve, and our suggestion is to wipe dry every morning, open windows to air the room and to review curtaining arrangements – the curtains here drew across the

Fig 3.15 Damp and mould in corner of a room caused by condensation.

BELOW LEFT: Fig 3.16 Condensation and mould forming below a bay window at the coldest places in the room. Note that the bottom of the skirting is cold. This is because there isn't anything sealing the floor to the wall to prevent draughts.

whole bay, leaving it considerably colder than the room. There was also evidence of mould on the window frame and glazing gasket.

Where mould grows on a ceiling, residents are often convinced this is because of a roof leak but, as in Fig 3.18, it can simply be a patch of missing loft insulation. In this case, it meant that small area of ceiling was colder than anywhere else in the room so condensation was forming there, and over a period of time mould was able to take a hold. Replacing a very small patch of insulation solved the problem completely and it didn't return after the ceiling was sterilised and repainted.

Fig 3.17 Mould growing on the sealant in the corner of a bay window.

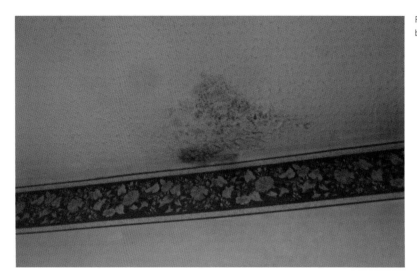

Fig 3.18 Mould patch on a bedroom ceiling.

Opening Windows

When it is not windy your windows will need to be open wider when you wish to ventilate your home: on a calm day you should open them fully. This should happen every morning for twenty minutes for bedrooms that are in use. If it is windy, you can reduce the time as well as how far the windows are open; for instance, when it's blowing a gale, you may only need to open the window a tiny crack because a lot of air will be rushing in, and the room might be fully ventilated within five minutes. In average conditions, you might open one window half or a third of the way, depending on the speed and direction of the wind. With experience you will get to know how much you need to open your windows in various conditions to ventilate the rooms.

We call this type of ventilation 'purge ventilation' and it's very important for other rooms too. If you've been boiling food in the kitchen or you've burnt the toast, purge ventilation is a very good way of refreshing the air. You might even open the front and back doors and blow the place through.

OPPOSITE BOTTOM, AND THIS PAGE: Figs 3.19–3.24 Windows being progressively opened depending on how windy or calm it is.

Sliding Sash Windows

With sliding sash windows, the same principle applies and different degrees of opening will be required depending on how windy it is and how much ventilation is needed. How long the window is open can also be varied as necessary.

FAR LEFT: Fig 3.25 Window in the secure ventilate position.

LEFT: Fig 3.26 A double-position latching plate. The first position on it is for fully closed and the second offers secure ventilation. In summer, the windows can be kept cracked open in the second position, as shown in Fig 3.25, to help keep the room cool and well-ventilated.

OPPOSITE LEFT AND ABOVE: Figs 3.27 and 3.28 A sliding sash window in the closed position. The stick is there as the sash weight hits the bottom of the sash box before the sash gets to the top.

Figs 3.29 and 3.30 Sash window open a little bit at the top.

Figs 3.31 and 3.32 Sash window open a lot at the top – in summer or for purge ventilation.

Figs 3.33 and 3.34 Maximum ventilation can be achieved by opening both the top and bottom sashes together like this. The bottom sash should be restricted to opening a maximum of 100mm if there is any possibility of small children having access to the window. This can be done by fixing a block of wood or a rubber door stop 100mm above the top of the bottom sash in the runway.

Pipes Through Ceilings

Draughts can often get through where holes have been left around pipes, especially those that have been installed or moved after the construction of the building.

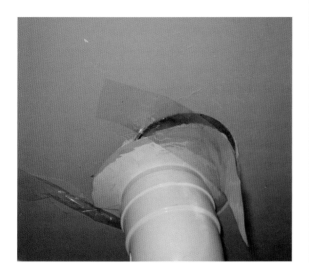

Fig 3.9 This boiler flue pipe may have been moved and/or the boiler or flue replaced, leaving a draughty hole in the ceiling.

Figs 3.10 and 3.11 Typically, we always find holes around pipes through airing cupboard ceilings like these, as well as holes where pipes have been taken out, and holes and gaps round wires.

Fig 3.12 This is an extreme case of holes left in an airing cupboard ceiling. We regularly find holes like these.

Chapter Four

How Insulation Works

In this chapter we will look at the different types of insulation that are available, which ones are the most economical to use and in what situations. Some consideration will be given to which ones are easiest to fit and how to compare different insulation thicknesses. We will consider insulation strategies for various scenarios, including for new builds, renovations and extensions.

We want our homes to be warm and comfortable, and insulation helps us achieve this. In winter, when it's cold, heat is continuously trying to escape from our homes, including some of the heat that we have generated inside the home. If we add a layer of insulation between us and the outside world, rather like wearing a pullover and thick coat if we're going out when it's cold, then we will reduce the heat loss from our home and this in turn reduces our heating costs. In summer, when it is too warm, we like to keep heat out of our homes and insulation can help do this for us too. Good insulation does both things – it keeps us warm in winter and cool in summer.

We need to be careful not to have too much glazing. South- and/or west-facing windows and patio doors need to be carefully designed as they can cause overheating in the summer. My best advice to mitigate this overheating is to shade your windows and patio doors externally. If you can stop the heat getting into your home in the summer, then you've won a good part of the battle against overheating.

How does Insulation Work?

Thermal insulation is a means of preventing heat loss or heat gain by creating a barrier between two places that have significantly different temperatures. By using insulation in your home, you can reduce heat loss during cold weather and keep your home cool during periods of warm weather, reducing your bills at the same time. The economic advantages, cost benefits and payback times of insulation works have all recently improved radically due to the 2022 energy price hike.

Insulation is not designed to keep the cold out but to slow the loss of heat from the building. Depending on the situation, heat can be lost in many different ways, including through shared walls with adjoining buildings, or through the floor in a flat. In a typical house, as much as 30 per cent of your heat can be lost through the walls and 20–25 per cent through the roof. Therefore the main areas that you should consider for insulation are the roof, walls and floors.

You cannot completely eradicate heat loss, but you can do your best to reduce it by insulating. For both insulation that is added at the time of construction and that is upgraded later, we often talk about payback times, cost-effectiveness and returns on investment, but bear in mind it is always going to be much more expensive to upgrade retrospectively at a later point in time.

In most cases, installing insulation will not require planning permission. We use something called a U-value to quantify the amount of heat that will be lost through a building element. Current regulations require a U-value of 0.13 W/m^2-K for floors and roofs and 0.18 W/m^2-K for walls; for refurbishments the requirements are slightly less rigorous. I don't find any of them particularly stringent, however, and have always encouraged my clients to treat the regulations as a minimum standard to exceed them, rather than aiming just to scrape through.

Unfortunately, the latter tends to be the prevailing philosophy among the major housebuilders, architects and designers. Therefore new homes that are being built often fall short of the standard that the design intended. We call this shortfall 'the performance gap' – the difference between theory and what happens in practice. Were new homes to be tested, their U-values as built would be significantly less in the real world than they should have been according to the plans and designs.

Loft Insulation

I hope you have insulation in your loft – but how much have you got there? 100mm? 200mm? 270mm? The latter is the current building regulation standard requirement. We now suggest 400mm, but for my own house I installed 500mm, and in many parts of the loft I have 600mm. In the walls I have 300mm and, where the walls meet the roof, I designed it so that there is 400mm of insulation in the wall plate zone, while still allowing clear air space above the insulation there for ventilation. My house is effectively wearing a thick thermal jacket. All this extra

Living Without a Heating System

In the winter, the idea of living without a heating system would seem unthinkable to most people. It is totally possible, however, and I've been living without one for the last twelve years. We are never cold as the house was designed to be habitable without additional heating as long as outdoor temperatures don't go below −3°C, a very rare event where I live. Strangely, in the first few years that I lived in the house, we had temperatures of −6°, −9° and −11°. When it was cold like that, we just put on a small convector heater, which, even when it was very cold, only consumed 60W when it was −6° outside and 300W when it was −11°.

So how did I create a house like that? I based my design on the Saskatchewan Eco House, which was built in 1977 in Regina in Canada. It was designed as a test case for a very low-energy home, with evacuated tube solar panels, quadruple glazing, a heat recovery ventilation system, passive solar design and a raft of other features that we would now call eco-design objectives. The upshot of their research was that a house didn't need a heating system unless temperatures regularly fell below −3° in winter, exactly what

we have in England. Unfortunately, this research fell on deaf ears until I picked it up and used it to build my house. I started in 2008, completed it in 2009 after eight months of hard work, and have been living in it without a formal heating system ever since.

My target U-values for walls and roof were 0.1 W/m^2-K, that is, watts per square metre per degree Kelvin (Kelvin degrees are the same as degrees centigrade). All the windows were triple glazed with special solar capture glass; Xenon gas filling was used in the south facing ones to maximise winter solar gain; their U-value was 0.7 W/m^2-K. My airtightness target was less than one air change per hour at 50 Pa, and a heat-recovery ventilation system was a key part of the plan so that heat could be recovered from the outgoing air stream.

Two friends checked out my design using thermal models or building physics models and they were both in agreement that I could indeed live without a heating system, which was my aim. I chose to use the cheapest materials possible for insulation (fibreglass). Throughout the book, I will often be recommending insulation based on my experiences and guided by economics.

insulation only cost me about £1,200 more than it would have if I had merely built to the current building regulations standard required at the time. However, it has saved me much more than that in heating bills each year.

You may be surprised at the suggestion that you should have 400mm of insulation in your loft but it is not difficult to achieve.

Where should a roof be insulated – at ceiling level or at roof rafter level? In recent years, loft insulation seems to have moved to some extent from ceiling to roof rafter level. If the loft insulation runs up and down the rafters, there will be a 40 per cent larger area of insulation and consequently a 40 per cent greater heat loss. That does not include the area of the gable walls, if there are any; if we do include this, then the additional areas of insulation are much greater and we are looking at a 60–75 per cent or greater upward heat loss for most homes. In the special case of hipped roofs (where there are no gables), the loss is just 40 per cent as there are no gables to lose heat through. All these calculations assume that the loft itself is airtight, whereas in practice it almost certainly won't be. This factor on its own should rule out installation at rafter level, and yet it often doesn't.

My strong recommendation is to insulate a loft at ceiling level.

Installing Loft Insulation

The simplest method to insulate a loft is to roll out a fibreglass or mineral wool quilt. The first layer should be about the same thickness as the ceiling joists and go between them. The next layer should go at right angles to this and should build the thickness of the loft insulation up to 400mm. Usually there will be 100mm between the ceiling joists and a further 300mm across the joists at right angles to them. There must not be any gaps between pieces of insulation, no gap around the perimeter and no gap between the ends or the sides of the quilt.

Many of you will have storage areas in your lofts. The easiest thing is just to insulate around them; that will do quite a lot of good. For a more comprehensive

ABOVE LEFT: Fig 4.1 A shallow-pitched roof where blown-in insulation has been used. It probably blocks ventilation at the eaves, but the loft looks to be in good condition.

ABOVE RIGHT: Fig 4.2 This is an older roof that has no sarking membrane or roofing felt, which is good as it means that the roof will be very well ventilated. It appears there's only 75mm of loft insulation, so it could really do with topping up. We can almost see sloping soffits running a little bit down below the level of the ceiling tie; that area looks like it's not insulated at all.

Warm and Cold Roofs

A **warm roof** is where there is no insulation on the ceiling, but has been added above the top of the rafters. In a **cold roof** the insulation is on top of the ceiling.

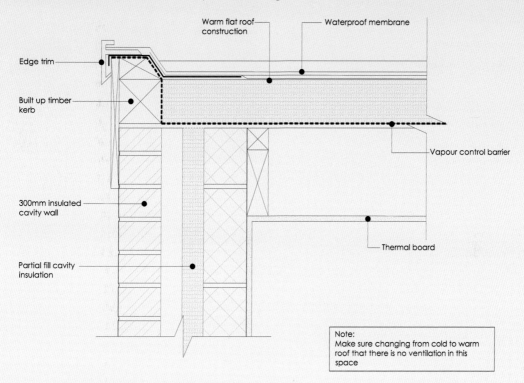

Warm flat roof construction — Waterproof membrane

Edge trim

Built up timber kerb

Vapour control barrier

300mm insulated cavity wall

Thermal board

Partial fill cavity insulation

Note:
Make sure changing from cold to warm roof that there is no ventilation in this space

Fig 4.3 Section through a warm roof. It is very important that no outdoor air or wind can enter the void in such a roof but sadly it often does, especially if it started out as a cold roof.

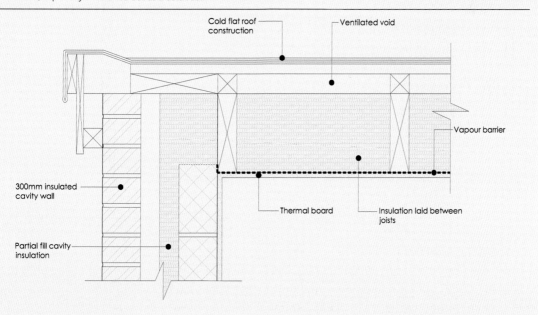

Cold flat roof construction — Ventilated void

Vapour barrier

300mm insulated cavity wall

Thermal board — Insulation laid between joists

Partial fill cavity insulation

Fig 4.4 Section through a cold roof.

Fig 4.5 Insulation missing between the first ceiling joist and the wall. This is a very common problem.

Fig 4.6 Building an extension in line with the existing roof. It was very brave to use trusses! We got it right and everything lined up perfectly. Our build process was to have the trusses up and braced, tack the ceiling, insulate, felt and batten, then come back the next day and tile it. Now I would be very concerned about the thermal bridging of all three of the gable walls.

Natural Insulation

You might be thinking about using sheep's wool instead of the inorganic quilts, but a word of caution – it is very expensive and there are some downsides to using it. It normally comes treated to prevent infestation by insects, but problems have occurred where this treatment didn't work. Moths can eat sheep's wool and other insects love living in it.

job, however, insulate the whole loft to a good thickness and then reinstall the storage deck with a 50mm clear gap above the top of the insulation so that air can flow through this space and remove any dampness that might come up through or out of the insulation. In very cold weather, if you go up into your loft early in the morning you will see tiny droplets of water sitting on top of your insulation, exactly like dew on the grass in the morning. This soon evaporates as the loft warms up in the sun and it's not a problem unless it soaks into the underneath of your storage deck and mould starts to form.

In my loft I used little uprights sitting on top of the roof trusses every 800mm or 900mm to support the 50mm × 47mm bearers on which my roof deck sits. I do not have any problems with damp, mould

or condensation. I have a continuous vapour barrier between the ceiling plasterboard and the insulation. This also acts as an airtightness layer, and I have plastered it into the top of the walls, forming a hermetic seal with them, so there can be no draughts coming in or going out at the edges of the ceiling anywhere.

If your loft isn't insulated to a sufficiently high standard, you may wish to employ someone to insulate it for you. This will usually only take a couple of hours for them to do. You should ask them what they are going to do to maintain eave ventilation in your loft. This is very important, as insulation must not block air flow from the eaves. Sometimes special plastic trays are used at the eaves to form a gap between the top of the insulation and the underside of your sarking felt; alternatively, they will cut the insulation to an angle to match the roof and slide it in, leaving a gap for ventilation. The worst possible scenario is that they miss out insulation at the eaves. I always recommend inspecting the work before paying them.

For a good result, you should clear your loft of any items stored there before the workpeople arrive to do the job and make sure that any tanks and pipes are insulated. When they have gone, think carefully about what you want to keep up in the loft and try to thin down the amount of stuff if possible.

Sloping Soffits and Galleried Ceilings

Sloping soffits and galleried ceilings are very difficult to insulate retrospectively; the best time to do them is while the roof coverings are removed, as then insulation can be added very easily from above. This would be my recommended way of insulating both sloping soffits and galleried ceilings.

If you want to try to insulate a sloping soffit, by which I mean a soffit varying between a few hundred millimetres long up to say a metre, then you're up against a problem which is very difficult to solve. The reason for this is that you need to leave a gap for ventilation. In theory, it can be done by sliding sheet insulation down from the main loft above it into the gap, but in practice this is virtually impossible, because the roof rafter and the ceiling joist overlap at the point where you're going to be trying to push the insulation down; you have to push down a piece that's too narrow for the space, followed by another narrow piece to make up the gap, at the same time as trying to keep them in contact with the ceiling and the rafter on each side. If they are not in contact with the ceiling, they might as well not be there.

The way I have tackled this issue in the past is effective but technically does not comply with the regulations, so it should not be considered as a recommendation. I take a ball of fibreglass quilt and push it down to the bottom of the sloping soffit void, jamming it between the wall plate and the sarking felt or battens. I then pour polystyrene beads down the gap and fill it completely. Remarkably, it does work, although I do feel sorry for the roofer who comes along to reroof and finds polystyrene beads blowing everywhere. When this happened to me, I swept them up and collected them in bags and reused them. At the top of the filled sloping soffit, I use the end of a length of fibreglass quilt to cover up the beads to stop them blowing around in the wind.

I then ventilate the remainder of the loft from there on upwards, sometimes installing through tile vents but often putting something between the sarking felt where it overlaps the sheet below so that the overlap is open and allows ventilation of the roof void. At the ridge I do something similar, sometimes cutting small slots into the sarking felt to add ventilation to the roof. There are proprietary ventilators that can be installed through the sarking felt to facilitate ventilation, but I find gaps or slots work perfectly well.

It is very important to ventilate lofts and the work described above may be covered in the regulations by a caveat that allows 'small areas of roofs' not to be ventilated. Usually, we would upgrade the loft insulation in the main loft as part of these works.

Walls

Walls are a lot more difficult to deal with than lofts, as there are so many ways of building them, and consequently a raft of different solutions to the problems of insulating them.

Let's start by talking about the modern cavity wall, which was introduced in the 1930s. Typically an inside skin is made up of either blocks or bricks with a 50mm cavity and then 100mm thickness of brick or masonry for the outside skin. Many of these cavities will now

Fig 4.7 It is not a good idea to store empty boxes or a broken cooker hood. Notice that you can see the tops of the ceiling members. These should be well buried under layers of insulation.

Cavity Wall Insulation

From the 1980s onwards, insulation requirements were brought in for all new-build cavity walls. For a while, this could be achieved by using aerated concrete blocks instead of breeze blocks or bricks for the inside skin, but as time passed, this became impracticable. The use of 150mm-thick blocks became an alternative for a short time, but these were unpopular as they took space away from the inside of the house. Insulation was added inside the cavity in various forms, such as batts or sheet insulation. Cavities were filled immediately after construction in a similar way and using the same materials that were being used for retrofit cavity wall insulation.

When a new cavity wall is constructed, there is an option to build in cavity wall insulation as work progresses. In many cases, fibreglass batts will be used and these will fully fill the cavity; this is my preferred option and is also the cheapest way of doing it. In my house I used 300mm of cavity wall insulation, three 100mm thick batts fully filling the cavity. More commonly, new homes are constructed using 100mm cavity batts and insulating blocks.

Sometimes sheet insulation is used in cavities. This is extremely difficult to fit properly and is rarely fitted well; any gap left between or behind the sheets will lead to a loss of effectiveness of the insulation. I have seen it done well by a friend who was a bricklayer and built his own extension. When he did it, he left no gaps at all between any of the sheets of insulation; all the joins were taped with aluminium foil tape. The wall ties were slightly notched into the sheets and taped round with the same tape so that there were no gaps or cracks in the insulation barrier. Unfortunately, this is pretty much never seen on building sites and, in general, cavity insulation is installed very poorly, leaving gaps, cracks, missing sheets and broken edges, all of which cause loss of heat and result in less efficient buildings than were intended.

Fibreglass or mineral wool batts can be used as partial cavity fill and a lot of the above problems will occur when this system is used. Usually, sheet

have been filled with one or other of the many forms of cavity wall insulation installed from the late 1970s onwards. For houses built after that, new cavities would have been filled with insulation during construction.

Unfortunately, 50mm or even 65mm of insulation is insufficient, so even if you have cavity wall insulation (CWI), it is going to be a good idea to add external wall insulation; however, for some houses it's not possible to add this and you may wish instead to add internal wall insulation (IWI), which is not quite as good but still makes a big difference.

In both cases, you need to make sure that there is no possibility of outdoor air bypassing the insulation. It is very easy to get air or wind coming inside from outdoors, particularly under the floor or in the first-floor void of your lovely warm, well-insulated home. Sadly it is a lot easier to talk about preventing this than actually doing so.

insulation is used for partial fill applications. The sheets can be made from expanded polystyrene, extruded polystyrene or polyisocyanurate. In theory, all these sheets meet the current regulations, but in practice, sadly, the finished walls fall far short of what was intended insulation-wise.

It may well be that in the future regulations will brought in that cavity wall insulation should not be built in at all but should be injected after the building is complete. Certain modern foam insulations are becoming the choice for the minor players in new house building already. My choice would be platinum expanded polystyrene beads, lightly glued together. In all cases much better inspection is needed and a major change of attitude in the building industry. As suggested, fail-safe processes would be by far the most sensible way forward. Post-construction testing is common in other countries but not even on the horizon in the UK yet. That testing is a standard part of the Passivhaus process, which will hopefully become a catalyst for change.

Internal Wall Insulation

This is where insulation is applied to the inside face of an outside wall. The least effective way of doing this would be to batten the wall and apply sheets of insulation over the battens, followed by plasterboard. A better plan would be to put insulation between the battens as well as over them and then fix plasterboard over that. An even better process would be to use sheet insulation, probably adhered to plasterboard, in a format known as 'thermal boards'. These can be stuck or fixed to the existing wall using special adhesive or foam, but I prefer to see them mechanically fixed in at least a few places with insulation fixings. The boards can then be either plastered or dry line finished and decorated. This work would involve removing skirting boards, radiators and electrical sockets and refitting them again afterwards. If there is coving, especially ornate coving, it makes internal wall insulation quite difficult to use, but it is not impossible.

You should set a target U-value that you wish to achieve and ensure that this complies with part L1B of current building regulations. Ideally it should exceed this standard by a considerable margin, as it is very expensive to upgrade the insulation later. I am not very keen on using things like warm cell or wood wool as they don't offer such good insulation values and greater thicknesses are required, which takes up more space. Draughts might also enter behind the linings, which makes the insulation less effective than it should be, as the insulating effect of the wall behind will be partly or entirely lost. These draughts can emanate from sockets, get into the first-floor void, or come out underneath skirting boards (much the same problems as we see with dot-and-dab plasterboard in Chapter 12).

External Wall Insulation

This is where the insulation is applied to the outside of a wall. In Europe, many new buildings are constructed using solid walls of either blocks, hollow-core clay tile blocks or poured concrete. These walls are then insulated externally, typically using expanded polystyrene sheets adhered to all the walls; these are then covered with a mesh and rendered, or an alternative form of rain screen is used to protect them. These same systems can be used for existing walls and the rain screen can be almost anything from wooden cladding to tiles, brick slips stuck on with glue, or a wide variety of the more commonly used thin high-tech renders, which more closely resemble thick paint but are breathable, durable and very popular. The latter would be the most economical finish to use.

I would like to see pre-finished expanded polystyrene panels that could be stuck onto the outside of buildings to look like ashlar stone. A new business doing this would be very successful. Some companies will come in and add external wall insulation panels with pre-fitted triple glazed windows to the outside of your home as a one stop shop for external wall insulation. Such methods might be used in the future on a massive scale to sort out the problems of poorly insulated homes. Some may also put on a new, highly insulated roof as part of the process.

Radiant Barriers

We're now going to enter an area of considerable controversy. I know this as 'the great multifoil debate', which is still the longest thread on the Green Building Forum and probably always will be. The debate is quite complex and extremely long-winded; you can read it for yourself at www.greenbuildingforum.co.uk/newforum/comments.php?DiscussionID=125&page=1#Item_0. The question is, does a layer of foil prevent heat loss from a building? Or even bubble wrap foil? Probably one good outcome is that foil is used on the faces of some insulation products. However, in my opinion, you need a decent thickness of an insulating material

Thermal Bypass and Thermal Bridges

Thermal bypass is the term used to describe the all-too-common situation where air, wind or draughts can either get past the insulation barrier or between it and the internal structure of the building and wick heat away.

A **thermal bridge** is an area that has higher thermal conductivity than the surrounding materials, creating a path of least resistance for heat transfer. Thermal bridges result in an overall reduction in the thermal resistance of a building's thermal envelope, resulting in heat transfer into or out of heated (or cooled) spaces. Some examples of thermal bridges are steel lintels, bricks built into aerated concrete blockwork, steel beams and their padstones, cavities closed with poorly insulating materials, chimneys and so on.

between you and the outside world, not just a thin layer of foil.

Gable Walls

When I built my house, the design included a large gable wall at the front. I agonised for hours over how I was going to mitigate the thermal bridge which would have been there if I had built an inside skin, which is the standard approach. The loft would be cold and then my inner skin would go from my nice warm house into a horrible cold loft and act as a massive thermal bridge. I could insulate it a metre up into the loft, but had I done that there would still have been a significant thermal bridge between the wall in the ceiling of my landing above the window and the loft.

What I did in the end might come as a surprise, especially to architects and building inspectors: I decided to omit the inside skin above ceiling level. I just have a single blockwork wall that forms the outside skin of my front gable. It has been there for ten years, and it hasn't moved. That is because I attached three studs to the front of the truss nearest the front of the roof and used them to tie the gable wall back

Fig 4.8 The gable wall of Tony's house during construction.

ABOVE AND RIGHT: Figs 4.9 and 4.10 In this loft it would have been preferable to lay the insulation across the joists. We can see that there's some insulation between the joists; below the yellow insulation is some that is slightly pinkish. It may well be only 50mm thick, so we would have laid another 50mm thick layer on top of it, and then put the new insulation at right angles to the ceiling joists across the top of them with no gaps or joists showing. There is a disproportionate loss of heat around where the joists are, known as thermal bridging, in this case taking heat out of the room through the joists themselves.

Common Signs of Bad Insulation

- The U-value of the insulation is too poor.
- Inappropriate materials have been used.
- There are gaps or spaces in the insulation layer.
- The insulation is not joined up with the insulation adjoining it.
- Thermal bridging has not been mitigated, for example from metal lintels or wooden joists.

Fig 4.11 Don't leave gaps.

to; I reinforced the truss structure with a few extra lateral and diagonal braces. Cathedral spires are built out of a thin cladding of stone that is tied back to a huge wooden frame inside the spire, so in a way I was inspired by cathedral architecture. In other houses, gable walls must carry heat out from the houses into

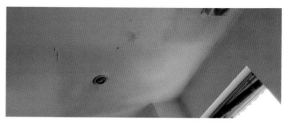

ABOVE: Fig 4.13 As in Fig 4.12, discoloured patches on a bedroom ceiling at the same property indicate cold spots caused by missing insulation.

LEFT: Fig 4.12 When these downlighters were installed, the insulation was not replaced around them, nor around the bathroom fan. Therefore the ceiling was a little colder and it picked up some damp due to condensation starting. This wasn't enough for moulds to start to grow but just enough for the surface of the paint to become slightly sticky and for house dust to adhere to it. The dark patches are dust and indicate missing insulation.

ABOVE LEFT: Fig 4.14 In the house on the left, we can clearly see the effect of heat rising through an uninsulated cavity and melting the snow around the edge of the roof.

ABOVE RIGHT: Fig 4.15 The end terrace house has a band of melted snow across the bottom of the roof, due to lack of insulation in the sloping soffit area, while the neighbours have obviously insulated their sloping soffits. The roof has a raised ceiling tie, and it's very difficult to insulate sloping soffits.

the loft. Chimneys do the same thing, which is a good reason to dismantle a chimney down to below the level of the bottom of the insulation when removing it from a roof.

Insulation Problems

We can learn a lot from snow on roofs. The pictures here are all very instructive, as they each show a problem with the insulation in the house being looked at. It is not always straightforward to interpret melting snow on a roof, but it can be a lot easier than trying to interpret a thermal image. Patches or strips of melted frost are often an indication of poor insulation; it's always useful to have the house next door for comparison.

In Fig 4.17 we are looking at one house with an extension. It is quite interesting that the loft on the original house seems to be much better insulated than the loft on the extension to the left, denoted by the line where the snow cover changes. We can also see that there's an area of melted snow above the line of the top of the existing former end gable wall. It's likely

Fig 4.16 This example is slightly more difficult to interpret, but it appears that it has little or no insulation in the sloping soffit; again there is a raised tie for the main part of the ceiling. It is likely that the snow melting on the gable is due to the sun shining on the end gable and warming it up.

Fig 4.17 Snow cover clearly showing the difference in insulation bewteen a house and its extension.

Fig 4.18 The house on the left seems to have a loft room with a very poorly insulated sloping ceiling. This could possibly be due to incorrectly fitted insulation with air gaps on both the warm and cold sides of it.

Fig 4.19 How many issues can you spot?

that there is no insulation in the cavity and that heat is escaping up the old gable wall cavity and melting the snow on the roof. A lot of trouble can be caused by heat escaping up internal cavity walls. One possibility is that part of the original gable wall was demolished, leaving the cavity open to the new loft, and that the whole new part of the loft is being warmed above the level of the loft insulation by heat escaping from the house up their old cavity and into the loft.

Fig 4.18 shows two pairs of semis with enough going on to write a dissertation about. The house on the far left has snow all over its roof and clearly has a well-insulated loft – either that, or the occupants are away on holiday and have switched their heating off.

The house next to it has a loft conversion and it looks like the sloping ceiling is not too badly insulated, but the ceiling above the front bedrooms looks to be very poorly insulated. There also seems to be missing insulation on the left-hand side of the new dormer extension near the main roof junction. This is probably where the staircase goes up.

The house with three solar panels on it seems to be well insulated, certainly around where the panels are, but then suddenly there seems to be no insulation above them. It is possible that the panels are thermo-dynamic ones and are therefore cold and preventing the snow on them from melting. It looks like there is a loft conversion with a very poorly insulated sloping ceiling; this suggests an awful lot of thermal bypass but it's very difficult to prove.

The house on the far right looks like it might be lacking a little bit of loft insulation because the snow has melted more than on the house on the far left. This could be because they're running their heating system much warmer, or more likely because they haven't got enough loft insulation.

We could go into far greater detail here on different types of insulation and where to use them, and there will be more on insulation in the following chapters. It's advisable to do your own research as well because every house is different, so it's impossible to give one-size-fits-all advice here. However, if you're going to do it, do it well: the additional cost of extra insulation at the point of delivery is small in comparison to the cost of retrofitting it at a later date.

Table of materials, R-values and suggested target U-values and thicknesses

Material	Form	R-Value	Ideal thickness (mm)	U-Value
Ceilings				
Fibreglass	Quilt	0.04	400	0.1
Walls				
Fibreglass	Batts	0.035	300	0.12
Rockwool	Quilt	0.04	300	1.3
Floors				
EPS	Sheet	0.032	300	0.1
PIR	Sheet	0.021	200	0.1
Lofts				
Sheep's wool	Quilt	0.05	300	0.17
Vermiculite	Loose fill	0.06	Don't use	
Other applications				
Aerogel	Encapsulated	0.015	Thermal bridges, say 30mm for window reveals	
Vacuum insulated panels	Panel	0.007	Expensive but to get 0.1 U-value 70mm	

Chapter Five

What to do First

Planning

First, think. Think about what you are aiming for. You should have a brainstorming session where you write down all the things that you want to achieve and then talk to other people who are living in the property, your friends, even colleagues at work, and pick their brains to see if they have anything to add to your ideas.

The second thing to do is to develop a plan of what you're going to do. You may wish to have several phases in your project and each of those phases should have what we call a 'scope' – the things that are going to be included in that phase of the project – which should be itemised. You won't be able to do everything at once, so you will need to choose what to do first. I can give you some pointers and ideas and then you can develop your own schedule; this may run over the next few years.

Before going much further, you must think about budget and how much all this is going to cost. You should prioritise the things that you would like to do first and have a rough guess at how much you think they are going to cost. My way of doing this is to do all the free and low-cost things first. Draughtproofing is low cost and has a very high return on investment. So long as you don't start straying into the territory of advanced air sealing, most of the things you can take on are cheap and easily achievable.

If the first phase of your project is draughtproofing, there is really nothing to stop you from starting right now. Begin by doing a survey (*see* Chapter 1), looking around to try and find draughts, and then work out

what to do with them later. I would suggest writing everything down in a spreadsheet, or as a list on a piece of paper, so that you can cross them off once you have attended to them.

In terms of which things to draughtproof first, I would look around for draughts and let the results drive your decisions. As a broad rule of thumb, I would do the front door, then the back door, then the loft trap, followed by checking the airing cupboard ceiling and underneath all the window boards. Next, I would check for any redundant air vents or air bricks, followed by checking around pipes that go through the wall or the ceiling, including the soil and vent pipe, which might go into the loft; this will almost certainly be boxed in and will have a gap round it that allows draughts in. Then go around all the windows: make sure that they have functional draught strips on them that are working; check the trickle ventilators to make sure they close properly and especially check that they are not draughty when they are closed. I would then look for any gaps under skirtings or between floorboards.

Loft Insulation

For me, phase two of the project would be insulation and this should be a priority. It is not very expensive to do, is simple, increases comfort and reduces heat losses. The next two chapters go into greater detail on this. Have a look up in your loft to see how much insulation there is. Usually, ceiling joists are about 100mm deep, so to save measuring it, you can just assess how far above or below the top of the joists the insulation is.

Case study – Terraced House

When the DraughtBusters were called out to look at a small terraced house in Reading, we were straight away surprised when we saw the condition of the front door. There was clearly a very big gap underneath it and the draught strips around it were very old and badly perished, so were not doing anything in terms of draughtproofing. A lady with a walking stick let us in. She seemed to be living in the downstairs front room, which that door allowed access to. She had a three-bar electric fire on full tilt and the sliding sash window was very draughty. There was no door at the back of the room, just a tiny hall that led to the stairs and the middle room and on to the kitchen beyond. She sat in a reclining chair exactly in front of the electric fire.

We had a look around the house for other draught issues and then we came back to talk to her about what we could do. We agreed that the front door needed to have a new sill or threshold and that the rear opening that led to the stairs should at least have a heavy curtain or blanket hung down over it. The sash window also needed partly sealing and partly draught stripping. There were various other gaps and cracks around the room that we suggested filling, including one where the telephone service entered her lounge – there was quite a draught around that and a large hole with no shroud.

The draughtproofing works only took us about half an hour, during which time we did hang up a heavy blanket over the opening to the rear door, with a restraint made from an old coat hook placed sideways to one side to hold the curtain back when not in use or when it was warm. We took off the old perished rubber aluminium carrier-type draught seals on the front door and replaced two of them with new plastic carrier brush seals to the head and latch side. We then fitted a draught strip down the hinge side. We always do this; it saves 40 per cent of the cost of the carrier-type draught strips and they are no good down the hinge side anyway; it's much better to have one that compresses as the door closes on that side.

The next day, I went back with a piece of secondhand oak, pre-shaped as a threshold, which was perfect for the front door. We bedded it on sand and cement and fixed it into the brickwork because there wasn't much left of the door frame at the bottom to attach it to. We also managed to fix it to the floorboard immediately inside the front door; this was good because it exactly lined up with where the old threshold was, and we sealed it as we fixed it. It sat about 20mm above the level of the floorboards, and we were able to perfectly fit a draughtproofing brush to the inside of the bottom of the door, which did a lovely job of preventing draughts coming in under the door.

The lady had been living in that room for five years like that and had spent her entire life savings of £3,000 on heating bills. When we left, she was so happy as she realised that she could sit in front of her electric fire with just one bar on and feel warmer than she previously had with three bars on.

Fig 5.1 Draughty front door with no threshold.

Case Study – Doing Everything Right?

One family did everything right, yet for them it had all gone horribly wrong. They had a shared equity scheme with a major housing association that placed all responsibility for repairs and upkeep, quite inequitably, on the occupier. The householders had prudently installed new windows and cavity wall insulation and had had the loft insulation checked. Their new windows upstairs didn't shut, leaving horrible gaps on the 'hinge side', which let in draughts and cold with the windows closed. The firm that had installed them had gone bankrupt so trading standards couldn't help much anyway. We arranged for new hinges to be fitted to solve the problem.

The cavity insulation caused problems in lots of odd places, with condensation, damp and mould. This was a result of the fact that it did its job in making the walls warmer where it was installed correctly, but any part of any wall that was not insulated or where there were any gaps left the walls cold, resulting in awful problems. (There are some more general issues with cavity insulation that concern me, particularly that it always stops at the top of the cavity, leaving an uninsulated section of wall between the soffit and the wall plate. I believe that this is in contravention of Part L1b of the building regulations.)

The inspection of the loft insulation, which reported that all was OK, was far from correct. For a start, the loft trap through which the inspection was carried out had 5–10mm gaps on each side and was itself uninsulated. The loft insulation was insufficiently thick, some bits were missing, and it did not quite reach the wall plate, leaving the edge of the ceiling cold.

These factors all combined to produce the perfect conditions for condensation and mould growth, resulting in very unhealthy living conditions. The family had done all the right kind of things yet were living in appalling conditions.

The cavity wall installation guarantee was used to get a survey which had to be paid for; however, when it showed that cavity insulation was indeed missing, the cavity wall insulation was redone properly. We returned to sort out the thermal bridging and missing insulation problems. We had also helped them sort out their insulation, condensation and heating control problems.

The issue with the windows not closing was temporarily dealt with by the occupants by wedging towels in the gaps; almost no cost savings resulted there – just a major increase in the quality of life.

The gaps around the loft trap will have added 10–15 per cent to the heating bill. Missing insulation at the ceiling and in the cavity walls, where it was only partially missing, will have added a further 10–15 per cent. At the time, these costs would have represented £100–£150 but in 2022 terms would be £750. The dangers posed by moulds are in another league.

Once you have done that, measure the area of the loft and you will be able to work out how much additional insulation you need to top it up, let's say to 400mm deep. Then search for good suppliers and prices.

The reason I've started with loft insulation is that it is straightforward, cheap, easy and quick to do, and makes a big difference. Usually, it will pay for itself within the first six months of the heating season if you do it yourself. If you pay somebody else to do it, it could take eighteen months to pay back.

Heating System Control

If you have a heating system, you should be controlling it using a programmable room thermostat.

These allow you to set different temperatures at different times of the day. For instance, if you set your thermostat to 18° for when you get up in the morning, this will save you 15 per cent of the heating bill during the period that it's on for, compared to having it on at 21°, as would have been called for by a normal thermostat. A programmable room thermostat will pay for itself easily within the first year.

The next step up from this would be an app-based heating controller that lets you see, set and adjust your heating from your mobile phone or tablet. There are even apps that will switch the heating system off when you leave the house and can be programmed to switch it back on before you arrive home. I love things that both save energy and are economic propositions.

Wall and Floor Insulation

You may wish to add insulation to your walls and/or floor. The cost of this will be significantly higher than for loft insulation, and you should get several estimates by contacting tradesmen. From there, you will be able to decide how it fits into your budget and when you are going to be able to do it. I never let tradesmen tell me what they want to do – I tell them what I want them to do for me. In many respects this is what we called 'scope'; it is a good idea to get several estimates for each job and a minimum of three of them (though it could be difficult to get more than this). They should all be quoting for the same thing, otherwise you will not be able to compare them.

It is worth investigating whether there are any grants that are going to be available; if you're in an older age group or in a special category group, there may well be grants you can claim to help with jobs like external wall insulation and loft insulation, or possibly replacing a boiler. Still possible but less likely would be the replacement of windows or doors. Were any of those things to be available on a grant then they should go straight to the top of your phase two list.

Advanced Measures

Phase three of your project might include things like ventilation, advanced air sealing or airtightness improvements such as sealing up the edges of the first-floor void, as described in Chapter 13, or doing works to seal up the draughts behind any dry linings as described in Chapter 12. Other possibilities are a new boiler or heating system, new windows or new doors. Most of these will be quite high-budget items but there is no reason why they can't form part of your longer-term plan. It obviously makes sense to do the things that are easy, cheap and economical first, but once you've done those, then there is the opportunity to move on to other things on your list. Replacement windows ought to be at the bottom of any list of priorities.

Checking Windows for Draughts

You can check to verify that your window and door draught strips work. We recommend closing a sheet of A4 paper into the window, making sure you have not trapped it with one of the snibs, hinge bolts or part of the locking mechanism. Then fully shut the window. Now try to gently pull the piece of paper out. If it slides out very easily, the draught strips are not touching the frame properly. There should be a considerable resistance to pulling it out. When I try this on my windows the sheet of paper simply tears, but my windows have four levels of draught seals all around every opening sash!

Fig 5.4 We tested this window as the sash was quite tall and these are prone to warping. The paper did move but there was considerable resistance when it was pulled, proving that the draught seals were doing their job.

Case study – Almshouse Bungalow

We were called to look at an almshouse bunga-low with serious draught problems. The occupant could only afford to run heating for a short time each day and spent most winter evenings sitting in his lounge wearing his hat and coat with his legs wrapped in a blanket. He was noting down his meter readings and rationing his heating to match his budget. This was so simple and so impressive I asked if I could take a photograph of him and his notes. He had open air vents in both his bedroom, at a low level in a door to the outside, and in his lounge, at a high level that we could see daylight through. They were probably relics from the 1960s. I blocked them to kill the through draught, having noted his new fan-flued condensing boiler and electric fire in the lounge fireplace. It seems all wrong to me that he pays over the odds per unit of energy simply because he uses a key meter.

When we asked for feedback, most clients felt that they were warmer and were able to save money on their heating. This client knew full well that he wasn't going to save any money as his budget was fixed, but after our visit he could run his heating for around three hours a day compared to the twenty minutes he could afford prior to our activities.

Fig 5.5 This pensioner noted down his meter readings to ensure he rationed his heating to match his budget. This may not seem to have very much to do with draughtproofing but it is a crucial strategy for all those struggling with finances.

Chapter Six

Ceilings

Draughtproofing

Ceilings are usually the most straightforward building element to draughtproof, as it is normally easy to see the whole ceiling. The best place to start is in one of your cupboards, or in the airing cupboard if you have one, where there may well be penetrations that go through the ceiling into the loft, often around pipes or wires. These can be filled round using acrylic sealant or decorator's caulk. Large holes may need some form of backing, such as a piece of wood or plasterboard stuck onto the ceiling above the hole where a pipe used to be. Do this from within the loft space; normal filler can then be used to fill and smooth over the original hole.

Figs 6.1 and 6.2 show some typical examples of holes in the ceilings of airing cupboards. Frequently, when pipes leak, when the hot-water cylinder is replaced or the heating system altered, a plumber or heating engineer may need to either add, remove or alter the pipework in the airing cupboard. Very often, this involves making more holes in the ceiling, taking out old pipes and leaving the old holes unfilled and draughty. Occasionally wires are added, and new holes made for these that are rarely filled. Sometimes bits of the ceiling can get broken and fall off. The

Fig 6.1 Typical holes around pipes in an airing cupboard ceiling.

Fig 6.2 Holes left in a ceiling after the cold-water loft storage cistern had been dispensed with in favour of a combination boiler.

heating engineer or plumber will leave it up to the homeowner to fix, and then nothing ever gets done. We have even seen the whole sloping portion of an airing cupboard ceiling completely missing.

Every time I look in an airing cupboard, I find holes in the ceiling where pipes have been taken out and the holes not filled. We always fill them. Some of these holes can be quite big and difficult to fill. They are above and beyond the call of DraughtBusters but we try to stop them being draughty by pushing some old carrier bags or rolled up polythene into the holes and explaining to the householder that they will need to get those filled properly later. Smaller holes (up to 28mm) can be filled using decorator's caulk. Small holes are easy, especially ones from 15mm pipes or where wires have been poked through the ceiling.

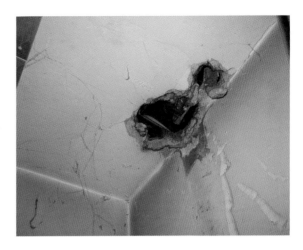

Fig 6.4 Major holes left behind after a rearrangement of plumbing.

Fig 6.5 Sealing around pipes in a newer airing cupboard.

Fig 6.3 Normal holes left after redoing pipework.

Always check the whole ceiling in an airing cupboard, especially the bit immediately above the door, as there can be holes and cracks there too. Make sure to seal around existing pipes, as they are likely to come through holes that are slightly larger than the pipes themselves. It is common to find cracks round the edges of ceilings in airing cupboards and these should be caulked in, again using acrylic sealant/decorator's caulk. I buy the larger tubes of trade decorator's filler, ten or twelve at a time, from a local decorator's merchant, as this is often on special offer. A slightly larger size of frame gun may be needed to use this size of tube.

Ceiling Roses

Ceiling roses are the disks from which light bulbs and lamp shades are hung. They are screwed to your ceiling and there will be a couple of wires coming through from the loft into the top of them. The wires are terminated in the ceiling rose and the pendant hangs down from it. The hole where the wires come through into the ceiling rose is big enough for a spider to come through and is also big enough for draughts, which is why we get involved with them. Even if they are not causing noticeable issues, they should still be sealed – every little helps. The modern guidance is for them to be sealed around with acrylic sealant/decorator's caulk. Very few people do this, but we do it all the time and we always check them. It is a very simple job and can be done by almost anyone, and certainly anyone with DIY or decorating skills.

Fig 6.6 Typical ceiling rose.

Fig 6.7 Filling the small holes around the cable entry point inside a ceiling rose.

A Brief History of Ceiling Insulation

In very old houses, ceilings were often made from round wooden poles with sticks nailed diagonally across the underside of the roof structure, followed by various types of lime plaster and attempts at achieving a smooth finish. During Victorian times, ceilings were generally made of lath and plaster – small strips of wood plastered over with a coat of coarse lime plaster, usually with horsehair in it. Then a finishing skim coat of lime would be applied. Although plasterboard was available from 1912, it did not become commonplace until a generation later; the building industry is hugely reactionary and very slow to change.

By the 1950s, plasterboard was almost the only thing used for ceilings and indeed it still is today. In the interim, various other sheet materials were used for ceilings, including thin plywood, Sundeala fibreboard and asbestos sheets, sometimes with the joins in the sheets covered by small strips of wood, and all painted. These ceilings were often draughty and, due to the era in which they were built, uninsulated when installed.

In the days of lath and plaster, no insulation at all was used either. This continued up until about the end of the 1950s, when small amounts of insulation were added above the ceiling. I can remember during the 1960s helping my father to spread vermiculite in our own loft, using a kind of gauge board to spread it out evenly, 20mm thick on top of the plasterboard, between the joists. I can also remember redoing it after high winds as it had blown around into what looked like snowdrifts; in places, whole areas of the ceiling were blown completely clean, while it was piled up above the level of the ceiling joists in others. Although fibreglass was available, it wasn't the product of choice because it was so dusty and itchy to use, and it was also more expensive than the loose fill material.

By the 1970s, fibreglass was becoming the most common product to be used for insulating ceilings. The typical thicknesses were 25mm or 50mm, although this gradually increased to 100mm in the 1970s and 150mm in the 1980s. Rockwool quilt became a popular alternative at about that time too. Although particulate insulation was still available, it was not popular. Cellulose fibre, especially in the form of fire-retardant recycled newspaper, did establish itself in a small sector of the market. The main reason for this was that it could be pumped into lofts more quickly and easily than fibreglass could be rolled out. Fibreglass could also be pumped into lofts in a similar manner, but this was far less common.

By the 1990s, thicknesses of insulation were becoming a problem and, although expanded polystyrene had been used internally, it always proved quite difficult to work with. It was being used as cavity wall insulation in the form of smaller sheets, but as the insulation requirements increased, the width of cavities increased, and manufacturers were looking for ways to make their insulation products thinner while still maintaining the same insulation value. The first step in this process was the use of extruded rather than expanded polystyrene. These products were sometimes also used as loft insulation.

After that, we saw the development of polyisocyanurate sheet materials, and a step change took place when these had reflective foil facings applied to them. These products proved hugely successful for insulating walls, skeilings (small areas of sloping ceiling that follow the line of the roof) and galleried ceilings. They were very expensive but still quickly became the main product on the market. Increasing thicknesses of fibreglass were required in lofts but, as this was a cheaper option, it was still widely used. However, quilt could no longer be used for galleried or skeiling ceilings, as regulations required sheet material to be used for all between-rafter and over-the-rafter applications.

Our suggestion is that you should insulate your loft to a thickness of 400mm with fibreglass or rockwool quilt. This is more than is required by current building regulations (though hopefully it won't be long before they catch up). Indeed, it may even be that thicknesses greater than 400mm will be required at some point in the not-too-distant future. Insulation is very cheap to install when a house is being built and very expensive to do retrospectively.

Installing Insulation

I have built a dozen new homes and over 700 extensions, some costing more than new houses of the same size. We would often build in this order: foundations, walls, floors, roof, ceilings up, insulate, roof coverings on (*see* Fig 4.6). Usually, ceiling wiring was also installed before the roof coverings went on. This did leave the plasterboard ceiling rather exposed, but the insulation was always done by lunchtime, felt and batten swiftly followed, and the work was fully completed by home time. The insulation was always perfect, wrapped over the wall plate and tucked into the top of the cavity. When standing on a scaffold, it is easy to leave a ventilation gap above the insulation where it crosses the wall plate. On the other hand, it is impossible to tuck insulation into the top of a cavity wall while lying in a loft. On my own house, I only insulated the wall plate zone (Fig 6.9) before doing the felt and battening, leaving the rest of the ceiling insulation until later, as I only had one person helping me.

The insulation on my house may not look very well tucked in but bear in mind that the cavity insulation consists of three 100mm batts. In Fig 6.9 you

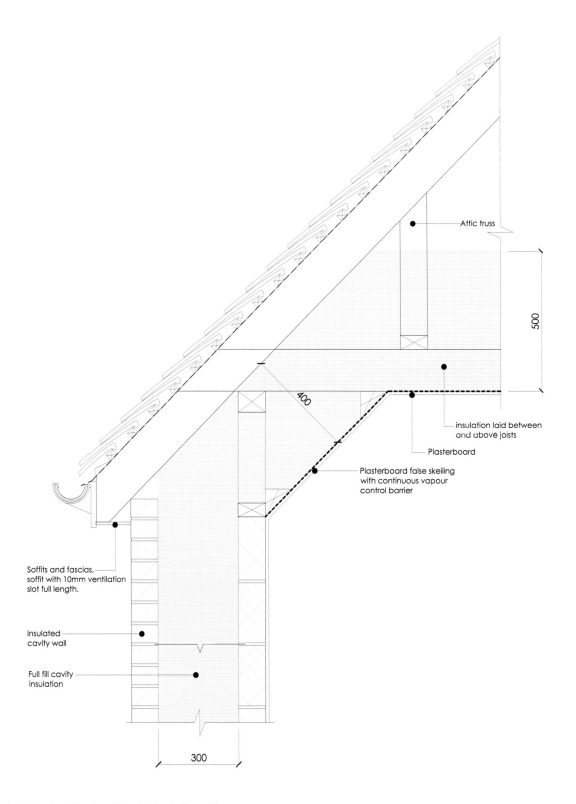

Attic truss

500

400

insulation laid between
and above joists

Plasterboard

Plasterboard false skeiling
with continuous vapour
control barrier

Soffits and fascias,
soffit with 10mm ventilation
slot full length.

Insulated
cavity wall

Full fill cavity
insulation

300

Fig 6.8 Sectional drawing of Tony's false skeiling ceiling arrangement.

Fig 6.9 Tony's roof insulation going into the wall plate zone.

can only see the outer layer. The insulation through the wall plate zone is 400mm thick. Note that there is plenty of room for air flow above this insulation. Some worry about wind washing of quilt insulants. I prefer not to have any membrane on top of quilts as moisture can condense in the form of tiny droplets and I like them to be able to evaporate away easily once the loft warms up.

Figs 6.11 and 6.12 illustrate an attempt to mitigate the thermal bridging at the wall plate. The plan had some merit but the execution was a disaster.

Fig 6.10 A whole pallet of insulation in the loft ready to use later.

Fig 6.11 Looking down a sloping soffit beside one of the roof trusses.

Fig 6.12 A slightly closer view of the arrangement in Fig 6.11.

The ceiling insulation was only laid to the edge of the ceiling and has been pulled back so that we could inspect the soffit. There is enough here for an essay! We can see that there is a rafter tray providing ventilation to the roof from the soffits that has built in continuous vents. Note that they stop level with the ceiling. We think that they should stop above the top of the ceiling insulation, which should have been 270mm thick on top of the ceiling (400mm would be even better).

Then the sloping insulation is only 50mm thick. It must have been bought in as a 50mm thick roll so may have been specified as 50mm but 100mm would have fitted better. There are gaps between the insulation and the plywood board that is there to support the

sloping soffit lining, so the 50mm of insulation quilt is doing no good at all.

The metal studs that we can see are forming a wall in the room below; if we look carefully we can see inside that wall, because on the left-hand side of it, the plasterboard comes all the way up, apparently to the piece of plywood, which itself is not continuous but stops and leaves quite a big gap before it gets to the truss. This gap can allow air and heat in and out of that stud wall. This is a very poor arrangement in terms of airtightness and heat loss.

You might wonder what the two long screws are that are poking up just in front of the edge of that sheet of plywood. They are plasterboard screws, quite long, and would have gone through the sheet

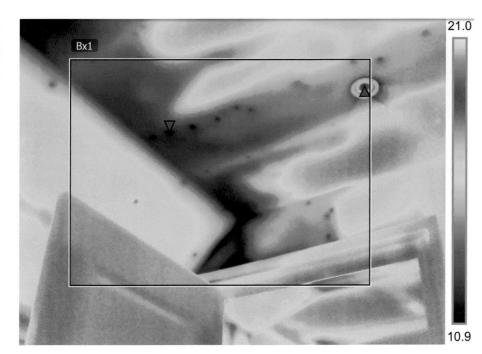

Bx1

21.0

10.9

Fig 6.13 Thermal image of the ceiling. The green and blue dots are cold screw heads. An internal partition should not be cold. The ceiling insulation was thrown in and wasn't touching the ceiling as evidenced by the blue, which shows that the flat part of the ceiling is effectively uninsulated at the edges.

of thermal board that has been fixed to the plywood. I rather suspect that in actual fact there might not be any screws going through the thermal board into the plywood, as it is stuck to the ceiling and the wall and the screws go through it at an angle, just into the plasterboard.

The thermal image (Fig 6.13) shows some screw heads as very cold and the internal stud wall as cold. The sloping soffit was warm but only relatively so, as it had some insulation on the back, whereas there was little or none for the wall, ceiling or stud wall.

Chapter Seven

Lofts, Roofs and Chimneys

Lofts are often the places where we find insulation. It is important that lofts are ventilated, because moisture from the house passes through the ceiling and insulation and in some cases condenses either on the very top of the insulation or on the underside of the sarking. In both cases it needs to be removed, and this is best done by ventilating the loft. Building regulations are very specific about this.

It is not easy to find uninsulated lofts, but every now and then we come across one. The loft in Fig 7.1 had a lath and plaster ceiling and is in a rear extension roof. If you look towards the front of the house, you can see a chipboard storage deck with a lath and plaster ceiling under it. There is no insulation there either, so the whole house had no insulation in its loft. It would have been losing huge amounts of heat through its ceilings.

Fig 7.1 Loft with no insulation at all.

Figs 7.2 and 7.3 A properly insulated loft with eave ventilation modules installed.

Fig 7.4 Well-laid loft insulation.

Fig 7.6 Insulated loft. We would have preferred to see the top layer of insulation laid at right angles, but it has been done well.

Fig 7.5 An uninsulated loft in a newish building. This one was forgotten about during construction in the 1990s; we saw it in late 2022!

Loft Insulation

I live in a house that I designed and built myself in 2009. It does not have a heating system, as I preferred to put in exceptionally high levels of insulation. You only have to pay once for insulation, but you have

Fig 7.7 Insulated loft with ceiling and stub wall of a loft room. It would be better to insulate over the vertical studs as well as between them.

Fig 7.8 Missing insulation at the edge of a loft.

to pay heating bills every year. My wall insulation is 300mm thick; this increases to 400mm as it passes over the wall plate area and is 500mm across the loft. I have a storage area in part of my loft and the deck is raised 50mm above the top of the insulation.

With so much insulation in my ceiling and walls, it was going to be crucial for me to mitigate the thermal bridge at the wall plate. In most houses, the wall plate only has a space of approximately 100mm above it, and 25mm or 50mm of that needs to be used for ventilation. Sometimes, when there are 'bird's mouth' rafters, there's only 50mm to play with anyway. I designed a false skeiling ceiling into my house so that I could have 400mm of insulation passing through the wall plate zone, connecting the 300mm of insulation in the cavity wall to the 500mm in the ceiling.

Fig 7.9 is from a good DIYer showing how he insulated his eaves box, the area between the loft insulation and the top of the cavity wall. You can see a ceiling joist poking out in the middle of the picture; the corrugated plastic roofing offcuts are being used as what we call 'eave ventilation trays': they are keeping the insulation away from the roofing felt and allowing a clear ventilation path for air to move above the insulation into the loft. They should probably have been a little bit longer.

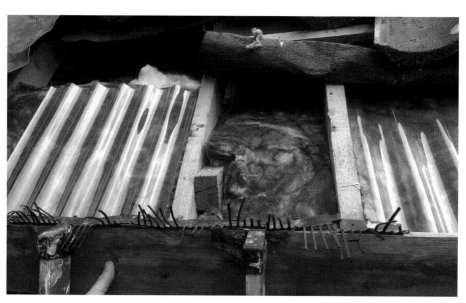

Fig 7.9 Retrofitting eaves insulation.

It is very impressive to insulate this area; most buildings don't have any insulation there, as the cavity wall insulation stops at the top of the cavity and the loft insulation starts just beyond the wall plate. In this case there were problems with condensation around the edge of the ceiling. This was the reason for taking some tiles off the edge of the roof and insulating this zone; fortunately, it was a bungalow. The yellow insulation is existing loft insulation, and the pinkish-grey insulation is being used in the eaves box to join the loft insulation to the wall insulation.

Wiring

Technically, wiring should go on top of insulation and not in it. It is all right if the wiring lies on top of or close to the plasterboard ceiling, clipped to trusses, ceiling rafters, noggins or whatever is suitable, as heat can escape into the room if the wires get warm. It is unlikely that lighting wiring would get warm these days due to the fact that the cabling will have been designed to carry 6A but will now be carrying only a fraction of that. An electrician should be consulted, and their opinion sought as to how safe it is to bury

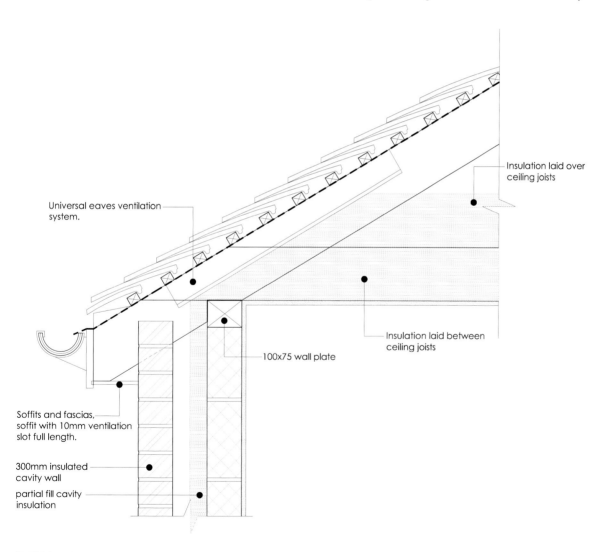

Universal eaves ventilation system.

Insulation laid over ceiling joists

Insulation laid between ceiling joists

100x75 wall plate

Soffits and fascias, soffit with 10mm ventilation slot full length.

300mm insulated cavity wall

partial fill cavity insulation

Fig 7.10 A typical detail of a 'cut roof', one built with bird's mouth rafters, where there is very little room for insulation. Although the cavity insulation is shown here and in Fig 7.11, it is incredibly rare to find any insulation above soffit level.

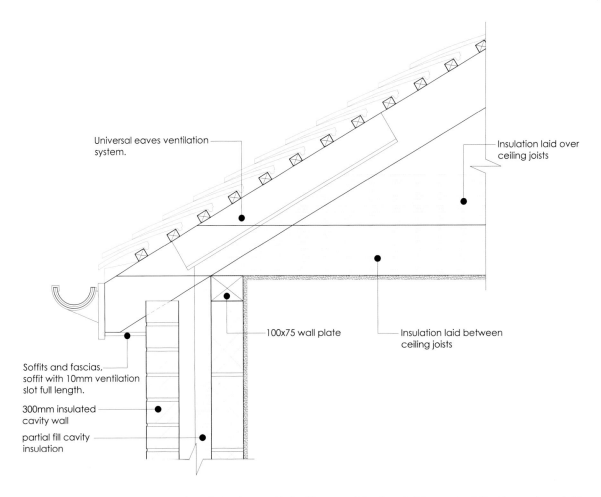

Universal eaves ventilation system.

Insulation laid over ceiling joists

100x75 wall plate

Insulation laid between ceiling joists

Soffits and fascias, soffit with 10mm ventilation slot full length.

300mm insulated cavity wall

partial fill cavity insulation

Fig 7.11 A detail showing insulation over the wall plate for a roof built with trusses. Often there is little or no insulation there and even built like this, there is insufficient insulation present.

lighting cables in insulation. Suggest that you wish to derate the protection for the circuits and see what they say.

You should not bury shower cables or cooker cables in insulation as they must be moved. Ring main cabling can also be downrated, from say 32A to 20A or 16A. Again, I think that these would then be fine even when buried in insulation, but do consult an electrician before doing any work.

Bay Window Roof

Friends of mine received a grant to carry out external wall insulation and loft insulation on their home, but the contractor did not want to insulate the front bay window roof. I could foresee problems if it was not insulated, with condensation preferentially forming there as it would be cold compared to the rest of the house, so offered to insulate it with some left-over polystyrene beads.

We started by taking off some tiles from the end of the bay window roof and opening a hole through the boards, then pushed a big blob of fibreglass quilt down to separate our insulation from next door's roof void and proceeded to pump in beads. When the roof was full, we made good the tiles, adding soakers and leaving it ready for the EWI contractor.

The building regulations that require ventilation in lofts have an exclusion for small roofs.

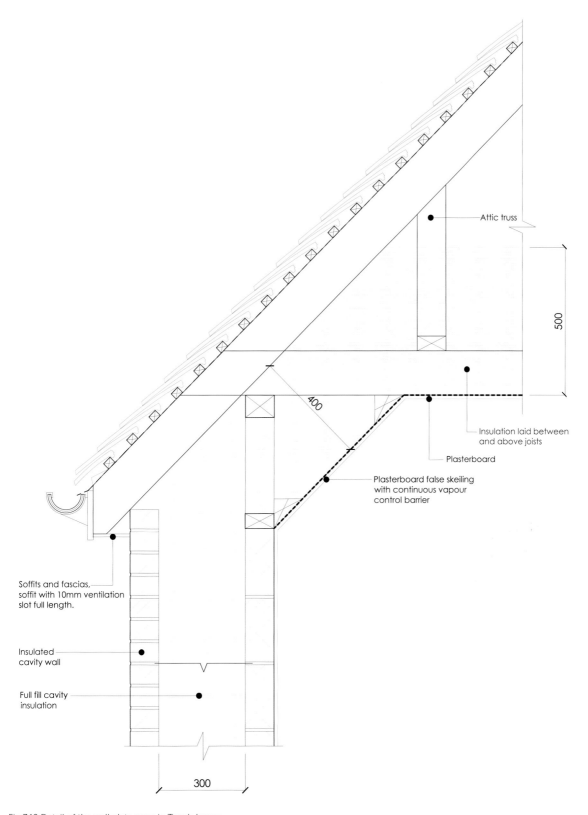

Attic truss

500

400

Insulation laid between
and above joists

Plasterboard

Plasterboard false skeiling
with continuous vapour
control barrier

Soffits and fascias,
soffit with 10mm ventilation
slot full length.

Insulated
cavity wall

Full fill cavity
insulation

300

Fig 7.12 Detail of the wall plate zone in Tony's house.

ABOVE: Fig 7.14 Some tiles removed from the roof for access.

LEFT: Fig 7.13 Inspecting the bay window roof.

Fig 7.15 Looking down into the uninsulated roof space.

RIGHT: Fig 7.16 Fibreglass quilt ready to insert.

ABOVE LEFT: Fig 7.17 Pumping in the polystyrene beads.

ABOVE RIGHT: Fig 7.18 The roof void filling up with beads.

Fig 7.19 Nearly full.

There can be massive problems with chalet bunga-lows and loft conversions in terms of heat loss, if any wind from outside gets in between the floor of the loft room or first-/second-floor room and the ceiling of the room below. The wind washes away all the heat that's there. In the summer, these voids can fill with overheated air from the loft spaces and make things uncomfortably warm at night.

If the floor joists run parallel to the ridge, then matters are less serious; it is when they run perpen-dicular to the ridge and/or when air or wind can pass right through the space under the floor to the opposite side of the room or building that problems arise. To combat the issue, the gaps between the ends of the joists need to be solidly and airtightly filled, in line with any insulated stub wall or sloping insulated ceiling above, and the insulation barrier needs to be joined up along its full length between the ceiling and the walls below the loft or attic room.

Loft Ventilation

Many homes have lofts with insulation at ceiling level. Where this is the case, it is important that the loft is properly ventilated. The reason for this is that on very cold nights, moisture, from the house or from the air trapped within the insulation layer, can con-dense as the loft cools down, either on the underside of any roofing membrane or on the topmost surface of the loft insulation. This condensation, in the form of dew, is not harmful, because the next day it all evaporates again. However, if the loft is not properly ventilated then it can't fully evaporate; then the next time it is cold it builds up again, and it doesn't take long for moulds to form, typically on the underside of the sarking membranes; it can also form on the roof timbers themselves or on any boarding or mate-rial that is close to the top of the ceiling insulation.

In Victorian or pre-Victorian homes, where no sarking of any kind has been used, loft ventilation tends to be so good there are rarely any problems; however, problems will occur as soon as the property is re-roofed and a sarking membrane installed, so at this point vents should be added. Up until about the 1980s, roofs were built without any ventilation, but insulation tended to be very thin; thicknesses only increased after that point. As soon as problems became apparent, building regulations required ven-tilation to be fitted to all new properties; somewhat later it became a requirement when homes were re-roofed.

Initially, soffit vents were fitted in the form of small circular vents, continuous strips of plastic with ven-tilation slots already in them, or soffit boards with slots or holes in them. I preferred to use 'over facia ventilators'; these were much easier to fit, cheaper and almost invisible. They did the job that was required of them. For some roofs it was also necessary to fit high-level gable vents, ridge ventilators or even tiles with vents in them to ensure that the roof was prop-erly ventilated. All this ventilation was required on the cold side of the insulation to keep the roof free from damp, mould and condensation.

Quite a few roofs have sloping soffit ceilings, where a small portion of the roof nearest to the wall plate slopes before it reaches the roof tie that forms the main ceiling of the house. These sloping soffits are notoriously difficult to insulate, mostly because they are very difficult to access. The perfect time to do them is while the property is being re-roofed. They can be insulated from underneath the ceiling by adding a reasonable thickness of sheet insulation (80mm), followed by plasterboard or perhaps more simply by a sheet of insulated plasterboard. If that is done, there is no need do anything further in terms of ventilation; however, if insulation is added above the existing sloping ceiling, then there is a require-ment to maintain some ventilation above this new installation. Strictly speaking, the regulations require a 50mm space for ventilation, but because it is usually a small area that is being insulated, a 25mm space is sufficient, especially as we recommend putting the maximum amount of insulation into that zone.

Flat roofs are not common on houses in the UK; however, they are very common on extensions and dormers. Again, where should the insulation layer be: at ceiling level (cold roof), or above the rafters (warm roof)? With flat roofs, however, these terms tend to describe exactly the opposite of the most likely situation, especially where a cold roof is converted into a warm roof.

When a flat roof membrane reaches the end of its natural life, which it usually does before it was expected to fail, a new roof covering is commissioned, sometimes involving removing a rotten deck and exposing the ceiling insulation. The works that follow are subject to Part L1B of the building regulations; these state that when you replace a flat roof you need to bring the insulation up to current standards. Now we have the problem of adding insulation to an existing roof. There often isn't space in the previous ceiling structure to cope with the present requirement of 270mm of quilt plus a 50mm air gap. In other words, are the joists over 320mm deep? The answer is always no. So now the roofing contractor decides to convert to a warm roof, where they can add a new deck, with insulation on top of it, and a new waterproofing layer quickly and easily. However, there is a problem with this course of action because the previous roof was ventilated. If that ventilation is left, it will be ventilating between the ceiling and the insulation. This is exactly the place that you do not want ventilation because it will be taking away all the heat that is in the room.

I'm a great believer in fail-safe design, and warm roofs are the epitome of fail-disaster design, as any air leakage between the insulation and the ceiling will cause high levels of heat loss. It is very difficult to make our homes airtight but at least when they're not, we know about it and can do something about the draughtiness. With a warm roof, it is incredibly difficult to put in retrospective airtightness measures, even if we knew that they needed to be done, which very likely we would not.

The Balance Between Draughtproofing and Ventilation in Roofs

It is not possible to over-ventilate a normal loft where the insulation is at ceiling level – these lofts must always be well ventilated. You should inspect your loft following a spell of very cold weather; if there is evidence of wetting from condensation, dew or even spots of mould or drips, recheck a month later.

Fig 7.20 An extreme case of condensation in a poorly ventilated roof. There was mildew on all the rafters and condensation streaming down the underside of the sarking membrane, soaking into the fibreglass and wetting the ceiling/ wall junction so badly that the occupants were convinced that the roof was leaking. It wasn't!

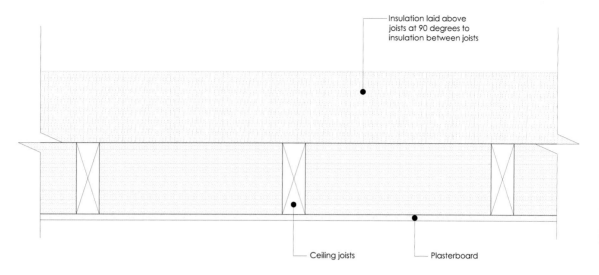

Insulation laid above joists at 90 degrees to insulation between joists

Ceiling joists

Plasterboard

Fig 7.21 Loft insulation as we would like to see it.

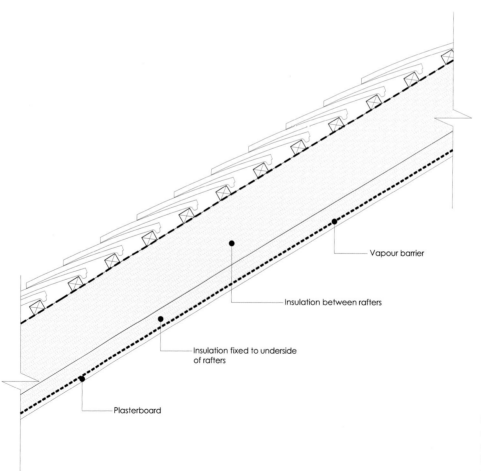

Vapour barrier

Insulation between rafters

Insulation fixed to underside of rafters

Plasterboard

Fig 7.22 Suggested detail for sloping soffits using the warm roof principle.

If the problems persist, add ventilation at both low and high levels.

In roofs where the insulation barrier is above the rafters, as explained previously, these voids should **not** be ventilated. It will be possible to check how well air-sealed the voids are in such roofs by measuring the temperature of the ceiling; it should be within a few degrees of room temperature during cold weather. If more than that, rectifications will be necessary in terms of air sealing the roof, eaves and gables.

ABOVE LEFT: Fig 7.23 A roof insulated at rafter level using a breathable sprayed-on foam. It is strange to see what looks like an uninsulated ceiling!

TOP RIGHT: Fig 7.24 Looking up the chimney in a bedroom that is now being used as an office in a terraced house, we can see that it is capped but there is daylight, and it lets a lot of heat out of the house. The householders now push a pillow in a couple of black sacks up the chimney in winter and take it out and store it in their shed during the warmer months. Last year they had their house at 20°C but this year are aiming for 19°C while they are working.

ABOVE RIGHT: Fig 7.25 Pushing a cushion wrapped in plastic bags up a chimney to prevent draughts.

The Loft Hatch

When it came to accessing my loft, the question was how to make a loft hatch with the equivalent of 500mm fibreglass insulation built into it. In the end I designed the equivalent of a porch into my loft trap. It has a very nice wooden drop-down ladder that comes with an integral frame and a plywood panel to which the ladder is fixed, and it has draught seals all around the frame. However, there is no insulation at all on the plywood panel. I would have needed to add 200mm of sheet insulation to try to get somewhere near the equivalent amount of fibreglass, but if I had left it with no insulation, it would have got cold and gathered condensation, which would then have dripped onto my landing carpet.

I had an alternative solution. Above the ladder and loft trap there is over 600mm of depth up to the level of the loft floor. I decided to have a second loft trap that hinges upwards; when closed, it sits on top of the floor, with draught seals that compress as the loft trap comes down. This was made from a sheet of orientated strand board (OSB), and to it I fixed 25mm and 50mm pieces of leftover foil-faced PIR insulation on top, and 50mm on the underside. The combination of a sealed air space between the two loft traps and the insulation on the top of the second one gives me the equivalent of the 500mm fibreglass that I have in the rest of my loft. There are no draughts at all through either of the traps or around the architrave or frames of the loft trap in the ceiling. I have a pulley and counterbalance weight to assist with opening and closing the upper trap and there are springs on the lower one. This arrangement is very unusual – one of the secrets of living in a very low-energy home.

Fig 7.26 Tony's loft trap seen from the first-floor landing.

Fig 7.27 Opening the first loft trap releases the drop-down ladder.

Fig 7.28 Door of the second loft trap seen from below.

Fig 7.30 The second loft trap door hinged open.

Fig 7.29 The air space between the two loft traps is tightly sealed.

Fig 7.31 The second loft trap door in closed position.

The reason that I raised my loft boarding by 50mm is that it is possible for condensation to form on the top layer of fibreglass insulation in a loft during cold weather, and it is important that this can be ventilated away. If the loft boarding sits directly on top of fibreglass insulation, condensation, followed by mould, can form underneath the boards. I was keen to avoid this possibility.

Your loft trap may be either a lift-out or drop-down one.

Lift-Out Loft Traps

Inspect the loft hatch. Is it clean? Are there dark stains round the edges of it, on it or on the door stops/lining? You should also look at the architrave or surround where it abuts the ceiling/wall. Are there cracks? These could very well be letting in draughts and should be caulked.

Now remove the hatch. Is it insulated? There is a better than average chance that it is not, and it should be. I like to stick a sheet of insulation on it. Thick expanded polystyrene is OK; I have seen fibreglass placed in bin bags and stuck on, but I prefer any form of sheet insulation. The aim is to achieve a similar U-value for the loft trap as you have for the rest of the ceiling. If the trap itself is dirty round the edges, this may be due to missing or ineffective draught seals. To apply draught seals, you will need to thoroughly clean the top edges of the place where the edges of the hatch sit. This is where you are going to fit the draught seals; these can either be self-adhesive foam, butyl rubber or nylon brush strip ones. I generally use E-profile butyl ones, and these won't stick to a dirty frame.

Note that if there is any blackening between the architrave and the ceiling, this indicates that draughts are entering there and that it should be caulked.

Drop-Down Loft Traps

Inspect the loft hatch as for lift-out loft traps to see if any remedial work is needed.

Now open the hatch, often a wooden sheet. Is it insulated? If it is not, it should be. Now, if there are no existing draught strips or seals, thoroughly clean the

Fig 7.32 Your loft hatch might look like this. If it does, it should be draught stripped and insulated. It should not have a smoke alarm fixed to it. The dark line along the top of the doorstop indicates that it is probably draughty; draughts bring in dust and dirt and leave them behind as they exit through cracks.

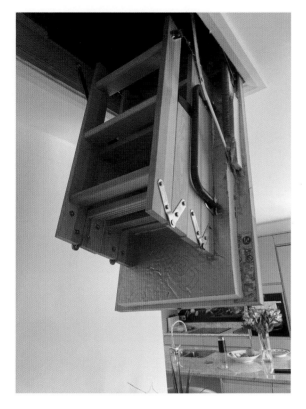

Fig 7.34 A loft trap without a ladder that shows a proper amount of insulation designed into it.

LEFT: Fig 7.33 An alternative way of insulating a loft with a ladder. An aluminium ladder would be a cheaper alternative to wood.

faces of the place where the edges of the hatch close. Apply suitable draught strips. Foam, butyl rubber or brush pile ones all work, but take care to choose the correct thickness. For the one on the hinge side, the strip should be fitted so that it is compressed by the edge of the flap – that is, it goes onto the member that the hinges are fitted to.

The hatch should have door stops. Many older drop-down hatches also have auto-latches or push-to-open catches; these are now considered dangerous, as they can blow open in high winds, and quarter-turn latches are recommended.

Note the thickness of the insulation in Figs 7.33 and 7.34.

Eaves Cupboard Doors

Some lofts are accessible from the living space in your home, especially in chalet bungalows or houses with loft conversions. These have eaves cupboards, which can be either inside or outside the insulation and airtightness barrier. If yours are inside these, you should check for draughts all around the cupboard; there should not be any need for either insulation or draughtproofing of the door. If there are any issues, then remedial action should be taken to resolve them. Where the eave cupboard space is outside the insulation barrier, any door will need positive draught seals to all four sides and will also need to be insulated.

Fig 7.36 shows an eaves cupboard door. We're looking down into the cupboard, and you can see that it's a loft because there's a roll of insulation there. Rolled-out quilt insulation is also visible. What else do you see in this picture? Stop reading for a few seconds and think about what you see.

What I see is that there is a patch of insulation missing immediately inside the door – the edge of the roll of insulation sits 100mm or so back from the door frame. It might seem a bit pernickety to

ABOVE: Fig 7.36 Eaves cupboard door with problems.

LEFT: Fig 7.35 An eaves cupboard door taped up by a frustrated tenant. We find these far too often.

worry about this but every little counts – why didn't they put insulation there? The next thing I see is that there's a little bit of darkening or dust on the room side of the door stop, especially at the bottom in the far corner. This is where draughts are coming from the loft into the room. There are no draught strips on the door stops!

Then there's no insulation on the back of the door. I've recommended that the client sticks 80mm or 100mm of foil-backed foam insulation board on this door. If you look very carefully at the bottom of the door frame, you might see that there's what looks like a drop of water, or at least a circle where a drop of water has evaporated. I strongly suspect that this door gets so cold in the winter that it gathers condensation, which runs down the door and then sits on the ledge at the bottom.

Another potential issue, not just with eaves cupboards, but with unheated cupboards and built-in wardrobes in general, is the risk of mould. I have seen a lot of problems with damp, mould and condensation in and behind fitted wardrobes and built-in cupboards on outside walls. The problem is that the wardrobe effectively insulates the wall from the heat in the room, making it colder and more prone to collecting condensation, which then causes damp and mould.

One possible remedy is not to fit cupboards on outside walls. If you do have them, consider leaving the doors open. Take plinths off free-standing fitted wardrobes and leave backs on, ensuring that air can get out at the top so that convection can effectively keep the wall behind the wardrobe from becoming too cold. In extreme circumstances, fit a small, low-powered tubular heater inside or underneath the cupboard on a thermostat. We have also seen heating pipes extended to run under fitted or built-in wardrobes.

Chimney Flues

Open fireplaces will be losing you heat: they help to cool your home!

Fig 7.37 Draughtproofing an eaves cupboard door.

Fig 7.39 Fit the missing threshold stop.

Fig 7.38 Measure the missing threshold stop.

Fig 7.40 Cut an E-section draught strip.

Figs 7.41 and 7.42 Fit the draught strips. Finally, adjust the latch if necessary and ask the client to add a sheet of insulation to the back of the door.

In the past, when chimneys were used for fires, the chimney stack would create a draw, which caused warm flue gases to flow up the chimney and out through the pots and away. The same thing still happens now, as the whole height of the flue is heated from the ambient heat of the home. Warm air travels up in a column and out of the chimney pots, driven by what is known as 'the stack effect'. If you ever get the chance on a cold day, as I have many times while working on roofs or chimneys, you can easily feel the warm air rising from them – it is quite considerable. If you cover a fireplace opening with a thin piece of cardboard or thick cartridge paper, you will hear and see it flex as warm air is drawn up the chimney. On a windy day, warm air can be drawn up even faster and, in some circumstances, cold air can whistle down a chimney too.

Reducing Heat Loss from Chimneys

All the following advice is for redundant and disused chimneys. Put a ventilated rain cowl/cap on the chimney pot. Now plug the bottom of the flue with a chimney balloon or similar. DraughtBusters suggest using an old pillow in a couple of black sacks during the heating season and removing it again in the summer. This will prevent most of the heat loss through the flue. We then recommend that you ventilate the top part of the chimney by removing a brick from each chimney flue in the loft at about 600mm up from ceiling level and replacing it with an air brick or fitting a plastic or aluminium louvre grille. Additionally, we suggest taking the loft insulation 600mm up the chimney breast, stopping it just below the air brick.

If the fireplace is on an outside wall and is sealed or bricked up or no longer in use, most of the remaining heat loss can be reduced by pouring insulation – for example polystyrene beads, vermiculite, LECA, perlite or similar – in through the air brick hole before fitting the vent or cover in the attic. This helps reduce heat loss up the chimney flue and is easy to remove (note that if an adjacent flue is still in use, you should not use polystyrene beads; choose LECA or vermiculite, as these are more resistant to higher temperatures and are fireproof).

If the fire opening is closed off, the insulation will sit on the slab. If you keep the fireplace as an open feature, a register plate will be needed to retain the insulation in the flue.

The Importance of Ventilation

If you just cap off the top and insulate the bottom of the chimney, 'pumping' will happen. This is where, in a closed-off chimney, the top gets very cold, condensation occurs, and the cold air falls down the chimney. Warm, moist air rises, which tends to dry the chimney breasts and indeed the house, but dumps water in the form of condensation at the top of the chimney, saturating it until it can take no more, at which point it starts dripping or running down the flue. This is akin to a tropical rainforest, except colder and not good. Adding loose-fill insulation will not eliminate this pumping action. Chimneys can act like dehumidifiers. With or without air movement, condensation is drawn to the coldest points, the pot and the flaunching, and can literally drip water that then runs down the flue.

An air vent does not stop this, but prevents it from being quite so bad; then, once the sun comes out and warms the loft (most days), the whole thing dries out with warmed, dry air flowing up the flue. This isn't covered in literature, but happens a lot in chimneys, so please keep at least the top of your flues well ventilated. Some chimneys have the pots removed and are capped over with cement flaunching; if yours has been capped in this way then we suggest inserting an air brick as high up as possible to add ventilation and help keep the chimney's masonry dry.

Chimneys on Internal or Party Walls

The best thing to do with these is to seal them up internally at top floor ceiling level and ventilate from there on up to try to keep the masonry at the top ventilated and dry. Insulating them is an option but is not necessary. This applies to all chimneys on internal walls – that is, fully within the building. We do not believe that an air brick is now necessary at the bottom in centrally heated buildings. Not having one will both reduce draughts and save energy.

Wood Burners

The stack effect can still work with wood burners, even when they are not in use. Warm air is continuously drawn through the appliance and up through the flue, dissipating it outside. There are several ways to reduce or eliminate this. One is to have a throttle or choke fitted in the flue itself; these are almost universal in continental Europe and can increase the efficiency of the stove; talk to your installer about installing one of these if you haven't already got one. There are many other ways of blocking up or reducing the air flow through a wood-burning stove. The minimum action would be to close all the doors and vents when they are not in use in the winter.

There should be a supply air vent somewhere in the vicinity of an open-flued combustion appliance, and this could be letting cold air into your home whilst the appliance is not in use. This must not be closed off, but we are hoping that some changes will be made to the regulations to allow a more common sense manual or automated approach to this problem. You may be able to decide on your own what you are going to do.

Chapter Eight

Walls

You might think that walls don't need draughtproofing. I wish that were true! It is often much less of a problem in older, brick-built houses, especially ones with solid walls. These are generally reasonably airtight as they probably have been wet plastered, floor joists have commonly been built in at first-floor level, and very often the ground floor was either constructed using wooden floorboards or the original wooden floorboards have now been replaced with concrete. *See* Chapter 9 on floors and how to deal with wooden floorboards.

Stone Houses

Much of the above is also true for stone-built houses, especially those constructed using the stone as if it were brick – that is, stone laid using mortar. Dry stone walling clearly will not be in any way draughtproof itself, but hopefully the inside of the wall will be. Again, wet plastering forms a very nice airtight layer. We have reservations about many stone-built homes in the north of England and Scotland, where instead of wet plaster, various forms of lining have been used on the inside of the stone walls. The lining is often constructed using battens and lath and plaster, or sheet material; in both cases the void can be connected to the outside air and the resultant problems are all those that we see with dry-lined modern homes, where plasterboard is either dot and dabbed or battened on. There will be a further discussion of this below, in the section on air sealing walls.

Dry Lining

With the advent of the cavity wall, we hit a massive number of problems that only we in the UK have. In most of Europe they build using solid walls, nowadays with external wall insulation; their basic structure is very airtight. Our cavity walls are nothing like airtight; wind commonly whistles around in the cavity and finds its way into the house through a plethora of small holes, gaps, cracks and spaces beside and above floor joists that have shrunk. Only the most diligent of householders tackle the problems that they cause. If the house has been wet plastered, then the problems are mainly in the first-floor void, and you can read about these in Chapter 13 on first-floor voids.

One of the worst developments in the UK building industry is the now almost universal practice of dry lining walls instead of wet plastering them. Wet plaster forms an almost impenetrable barrier to draughts, which can only penetrate where the plaster abuts another surface. However, where dry linings are used, the plasterboard is adhered to the wall with a series of dots and dabs. This inadvertently allows outdoor air to come in through the cavity via any of those small holes, gaps, cracks and breaches mentioned above.

Figs 8.1 and 8.2 show a partially deconstructed wall. Notice the dots of adhesive on the back of the plasterboard. The block wall that remains is the inside skin of an outside cavity wall; it is possible to see some wall ties if you look very hard. Much easier to see are the partially filled perp end joints; the arrows at the end of the wall indicate the joints

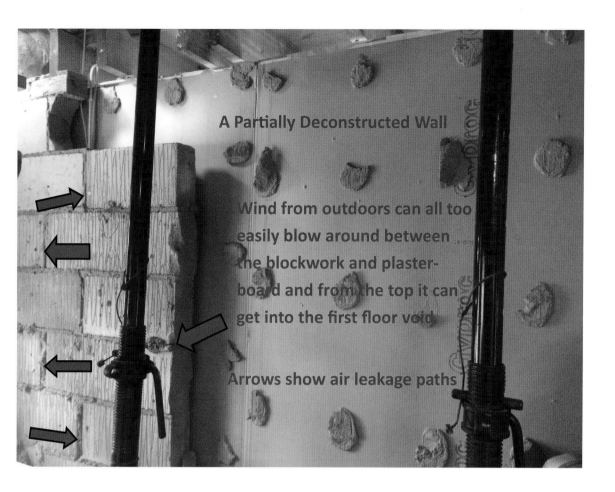

A Partially Deconstructed Wall

Wind from outdoors can all too easily blow around between the blockwork and plaster-board and from the top it can get into the first floor void.

Arrows show air leakage paths

ABOVE: Fig 8.1 Wind could easily blow in through the blockwork and up into the first-floor void. The red arrows point to gaps in the blockwork.

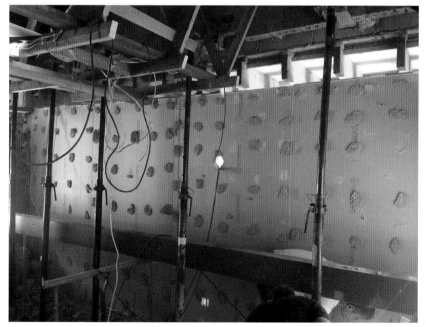

Fig 8.2 Looking at the back of the plasterboard after the blockwork has been removed, prior to installing a steel beam as part of an extension.

where there is no mortar or apparent mortar staining. There is a problem with aircrete blocks that the mortar can dry out so fast that no bond is formed with the block; this is especially evident on the ends of blocks.

For many years this continued to be standard practice, unchecked until it was realised that outdoor air was indeed blowing around behind the linings and people were effectively living in plasterboard tents. Then, no matter how much insulation was in the cavity or how well the dry lining itself was done, it was inevitably cold and draughty. The linings were applied by contractors who were 'on a price'. Even though guidelines were brought in that said that a continuous bed of adhesive had to be applied around the perimeter of all walls, this couldn't be checked and very rarely happened, so most walls, when examined with a thermal imaging camera, will show dabs of adhesive with no attempt at a continuous ribbon. The upshot of this is that dry-lined homes are very cold to live in and do not perform as designed or intended. The occupants finish up either being cold or having incredibly high heating bills. The issues are covered in greater detail in Chapter 12.

The illustrations below refer to a lounge extension, where draughts entered the bedroom floor void under the beam. From the cross-section you can see a clear air path to above the bedroom floorboards, with just the skirting trying to hold it back. Thermal bypass doesn't even begin to describe it.

One thing to note is that the beam sits above the ceiling level. I like that for aesthetic reasons, and, as a builder, always endeavoured to put structural steel beams above the ceiling. I pretty much always succeeded, surprising both architects and engineers; the customers loved it. On one occasion we hung a roof from a steel beam rather than sitting the roof on the beam. All the load was adequately transferred onto the steel beam, to the satisfaction of the building inspector. The beam sat outside the thermal envelope and there was no cold, draughty boxed-in steel in the new master bedroom, which had a completely flat ceiling.

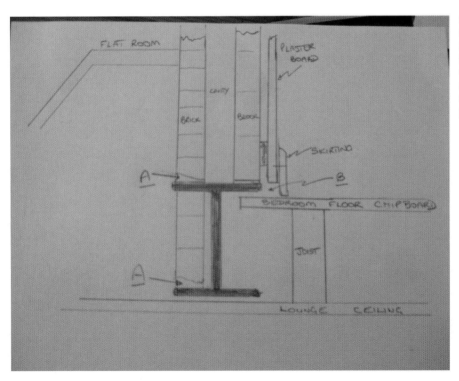

Fig 8.3 Here is a section through the RSJ above the lounge in Fig 8.4, which was installed when the lounge was extended. So many air leakage paths were built into this area that it would be difficult to add any more.

Fig 8.4 This is the RSJ shown in the cross-section in Fig 8.3. It was built in as part of a lounge extension, and there were air paths through it, under it, over it, round it and past it, all joining the new roof void to the inside of the house. The foam is the first stage of retrospective air-sealing works.

Sealing the Edges

If there are holes behind a skirting board directly connected to the underfloor void, this is virtually the same as being connected to the outside world, and remedial action needs to be taken.

We now need to consider the rest of the wall. The above actions will stop the air blowing in from the bottom but we need to deal with all four sides of every wall to make sure the air can't get in or get out from behind the linings. This entails sealing right across the top of the walls. There are two ways of doing this: following the procedure outlined in Chapter 13 for dealing with the first-floor void, or drilling a series of holes 100mm apart and filling each one fully with foam all the way across the top of the wall. We now need to go up all the corners, continuing the same sort of holes 100 mm apart and filling them each with foam. For this process we prefer not to use expanding foam but filling foam or adhesive foam that doesn't expand so much. Your choice of foam will depend somewhat on how large the gap behind the linings is: the wider it is, the happier you will be to use expanding foam.

The next thing is to deal with window and door openings. We need to make sure that no air can blow in from the cavity behind the cavity liners from under the floor, as we've seen in Fig 8.5. While we're at it, we need to prevent air from coming in underneath

Fig 8.5 Hole behind the skirting board.

Fig 8.6 Having removed the skirting boards, the gap was filled with foam. When doing this, you should ensure that the foam fully seals from left to right, including any gaps down the edges of the floor that lead into the sub-floor void, and the bottom of the plasterboard linings to the blockwork along its full length.

Fig 8.7 Surplus foam was carefully cut off with a fine-toothed saw in readiness for the skirting boards to be refitted.

Fig 8.8 The completed job. The room looks the same as it looked before the works were carried out but now there are no draughts.

door sills or thresholds. Around window openings, we don't really see it as acceptable to drill and fill with foam; some may wish to do this, however, because it's a lot less disruptive than removing the linings and sealing the surround properly, as detailed below, and consequently cheaper and easier. Our suggestion is to follow the process shown in Chapter 10, Figs 10.54–10.60.

There are probably millions of homes in the United Kingdom that are suffering from these problems. What we've just described above is a pragmatic approach that works to some extent and doesn't cost too much money. The real solution, of course, is to remove the linings and wet plaster the house, or at least all the outside walls of the house. This process is extremely disruptive and very expensive and so will probably only be carried out in a very small minority of cases.

We have come across many instances where new homes have proved very cold and draughty, and the owners have been tearing their hair out trying to get the builder or developer to rectify the problems. It is very difficult to get these kinds of rectifications done, and unfortunately all kinds of slightly underhand tactics are used to fend off claims. Inspections are sometimes carried out that find the work is of an acceptable standard, and everything happens so slowly that the people involved often lose the will to proceed. One or two cases in every hundred do get taken to court.

Many of these settle outside court, usually with a gagging order; we only know of one that's gone through the court system, which was awarded a settlement of £35,000. There were considerable costs on the client's side to get to this settlement, so there wasn't enough money left to re-plaster the house, which is very sad; however, this is now in case law so the big developers should be very concerned because it opens the way for other householders to make similar claims and succeed far more easily. Hopefully the result will be that the industry itself decides to stop using dot-and-dab dry lining altogether, although it's more likely that sales of parge coat, which should be applied as a thin coating to blockwork walls prior to applying linings, will go up very dramatically instead!

We haven't quite finished talking about dry-lined walls and how to retrospectively seal all the air movements behind them. Draughts can and do emanate from electrical socket outlets; these need to be sealed around. One of the processes is to isolate the ring main, unscrew the socket outlet, cut out 25mm of the plasterboard all around the socket outlet and fill it in with bonding and a light finishing coat over the top. Alternatively, sealing can be done inside the socket box using acrylic sealant, but this is tricky and not ideal. If it was my house, I would fill the void between the linings and blockwork with polystyrene beads or other suitable insulation material.

Wind Washing

Wind washing is cold air blowing into a room from behind the linings, as illustrated in this thermal image of a wall that forms part of a bay window. This case is particularly easy to see; there is massive air leakage behind the plasterboard from the top of the wall.

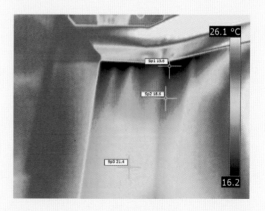

Fig 8.9 Thermal image very clearly showing cold air blowing in from outdoors and in behind the plasterboard linings.

Fig 8.10 Behind this bedroom wall, where there would normally be a lintel, we can see 25mm-thick fibreglass quilt dangling down. It was in the wall with a broken block sitting behind it, open to the soffit box; above the window there is a complete void that is also connected to the soffit box. This arrangement gives rise to a very cold wall in winter. The householder added insulation and ensured everything was airtight before repairing the plasterboard and turning it back into a bedroom.

Insulating Walls

The three basic methods of retrofitting insulation to walls are cavity wall insulation (CWI), external wall insulation (EWI) and internal wall insulation (IWI). The last two of these methods can be applied to solid walls too, with some caveats that will be discussed later. Cavity walls can be filled with insulation, but cavities are usually only 50mm or so wide and adding 50mm of insulation is nothing like enough. Compare this to the amount of insulation generally being used in central and northern European buildings, which is in the order of 200mm.

Cavity Wall Insulation

During the 1970s, we started to see some cavity wall insulation being installed by pumping urea formaldehyde foam into the cavity. There were many good outcomes from this process and houses became a lot warmer and much less draughty. There were also some downsides. Concerns were raised (mainly scaremongering) about a reaction between the resin in wood and urea formaldehyde and worries about it giving off volatile organic compounds as a result. The foam wasn't in contact with wood very much apart from the ends of the joists that projected into the cavity. Sometimes a little bit would flow around them and into the ceiling void if there were big holes around the joists. Then the foam is white and quite crumbly. It also shrinks after a little while and this allows draughts back in; it cracks a little like dried mud, but inside the cavity.

The last drawback concerns wooden window frames. Sometimes with windows it's a good idea not to paint the underside of the outside sill behind the drip as the window doesn't ever get any weather on it there; this allows the window to dry out by being able to breathe out any moisture that's in that section, a process that has been the saving of many windows. A lot of the houses that were cavity wall insulated in the 1970s had wooden windows and massive draughts in their cavity walls. These draughts went, to some extent, up and down the sides of the window frame underneath the sill and they helped to dry out the window so that it didn't rot. As soon as cavity wall insulation was installed, this process was almost completely inhibited, and windows started to hold slightly more moisture in them. They could no longer dry out by that route, and rot set in.

Over the next few decades, the CWI industry started to use other products to insulate cavities. Rockwool fibre, fibreglass fibres and polystyrene beads were the favourite choices; these all became very widespread and all of them have been used for new houses. In the case of new houses, the installation was carried out from inside the house once the roof was on and the windows were in. The cavity wall insulation company didn't need a scaffolding and they didn't need to worry about filling the holes back in again like they do on the outside, so there was less work to do. The installation was thus quicker and cheaper. It would probably have

Fig 8.11 Hole drilled for CWI, now filled with mortar.

been a good idea at that stage to mandate blown- or pumped-in cavity wall insulation rather than letting the bricklayers do it; there have been plenty of problems with missing or badly installed cavity wall insulation that could have then been prevented.

My favourite form of cavity wall insulation is polystyrene beads, as the fibrous insulants mentioned above can become damp and then slump. Polystyrene beads are installed with a very light adhesive coating, so they stick together and don't slump or move around. The best of all would be what we call platinum-coated polystyrene beads, which look grey and have a coating on them that increases their insulation value. Polystyrene beads work well in cases where water accidentally gets into the cavity or where there's driving rain, as they drain nicely and don't track water across the cavity, although the regulations preclude using them in areas of high exposure.

Fig 8.11 shows a tell-tale sign of CWI having been installed. You can clearly see in the middle of the picture that a hole has been drilled in the wall for the insulation to be pumped in, after which it has been filled in with mortar.

External Wall Insulation

This is my favourite method of insulating a wall. It is the best method as it doesn't involve any loss of space inside the house and it eliminates thermal bridging caused where internal walls run into external walls. This method essentially wraps a house in a layer of insulation. There are many ways of installing it, usually involving sheets of insulation. These are covered with a rain screen, which can be as simple as a modern breathable thin coat of render; other finishes include tile- or slate-hanging weatherboarding, and it is even possible to use brick slips to mimic the appearance of a solid brick skin.

Both EWI and IWI can be used to upgrade the insulation of cavity walls. In the case of EWI, the cavity must be filled to prevent thermal bypassing of the insulation, by either wind or draughts in the cavity or by convection currents moving the heat away up the cavity itself.

Built-in Cavity Wall Insulation

When cavity insulation is built into new walls as work progresses it is often not done very well. Gaps are left and joins may be untidy, folded over or missed out altogether.

Building in cavity wall insulation as work progresses can be carried out effectively. Figs 8.13 and 8.14 show 300mm-wide cavities with the insulation being built in during construction. There are a few things to note. Firstly, everything inside the cavity wall is neat and tidy. Although the building site itself is not necessarily tidy, there are no mortar droppings on the cavity insulation. The installer did try to overlap the cavity batts longitudinally, but it proved impossible to slide them over each other without wrapping and rolling the face layers, so they went in three at a time, butted tightly together. The insulation being used here is R32 fibreglass batts. The cavity is 306mm wide to allow the batts to be pushed down easily without pressing on the masonry and deforming it.

It's not entirely clear whether this is a cavity wall or whether it's a house built with a solid wall with 300mm of external wall insulation clad with brick. As basalt fibre wall ties are being used, I think we

Fig 8.12 Poorly done cavity wall insulation.

Figs 8.13 and 8.14 Wide cavities with insulation built in during construction of a new house.

have to say that it is a cavity wall, but in terms of energy performance it is far more like a solid wall house with external wall insulation and cladding. It just happens that a brick skin is being used as the cladding in this case.

Thermal Bridging

Let us revisit the family mentioned in Chapter 5 who had done everything right and yet had problems with damp mould and condensation all around the edges of their ceilings? Here we'll look at the problems inside the house and some pictures that we took inside the eaves box of the closed cavity.

In the 1950s, 60s and 70s, when cavity walls were first introduced, builders used to do something at the top of a cavity wall called 'closing the cavity'. This is where a brick is laid between the inside skin and the outside skin and quite often flaunched with mortar to hold it in place. This is a stupid thing to do because it introduces a cold bridge at the top of the outside skin and draws heat away from the house into the soffit box and outside skin. Figs 8.17 and 8.18 show how the cavity was closed in our example, probably in the 1980s or 1990s. I found it very remarkable that the property was built for a housing association; as can be seen, that action caused horrendous problems inside the house.

What we are looking at here is the outside skin of the house, which was of rendered concrete blocks.

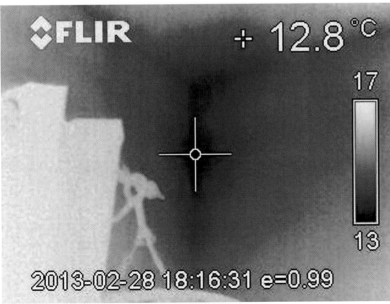

Figs 8.15 and 8.16 Thermal image and a regular image of a damp corner.

In Fig 8.17 you can see the batten that is supporting the inside edge of the soffit board; in Fig 8.18 you can see slightly more of the blocks. It's dark below them. On top of the blocks there are some bricks that have been laid and flaunched with a triangular line of mortar that goes part way up the brick. Then, behind the brick in Fig 8.18, you can see the aerated concrete blocks and on top of them is the wall plate.

The cavity walls were filled with expanded polystyrene beads. This had been done quite badly with a lot missing; an installer came back and injected these again, filling up all the voids in the places that were missed the first-time round. We then came along, took off the mortar and the bricks and insulated from the top of the cavity up over the wall plate and slightly into the loft. After that we tidied up all the loft insulation, joining everything up. This completely cured the problem with the condensation round the edges of all the bedroom ceilings and the bathroom ceiling.

Thermal bypass is when cold air from outdoors gets past your insulation, rendering it ineffective. By far the most common form of thermal bypass is encountered in dry-lined homes. These have plasterboard directly adhered to the blockwork walls. In theory, no air or wind should be able to get through a wall but tragically it manages to find its way from outside into the space between the plasterboard and the blockwork. The net effect of this is to cool the home. Draughts emanate from electrical socket outlets and from under skirtings, get behind the linings on internal walls and come out behind architraves. They are also able to get inside pipe boxings and floor voids.

In the case of IWI, thermal bypass can happen both in the cavity and behind the new linings. Some installers and advisers claim that this is not a problem when using insulated plasterboard, but we see this as a way of wasting any insulating properties that the structure of the house previously had. It is of course possible for draughts to gain access to other places inside the building.

Figs 8.17 and 8.18 The bricks that closed the cavity and caused the damp problems inside the house.

Severe exposure to wind-driven rain is also a good reason to choose EWI.

Cold Corners

The corners of rooms are always colder than the rest of the room. This is due to a geometric effect where two walls meet. Figs 8.19–8.21 show a corner

Fig 8.19 Damp in the corner of a room above the skirting.

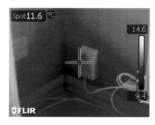

Fig 8.20 Infrared image of the same corner showing cold coming in from the outside.

Fig 8.21 Close-up view showing mould beginning to grow.

of a room on an outside corner, right down beside the skirting.

The infrared image is clearly showing some cold coming in through the telephone or internet connection in the plastic box. It is also very cold in the corner; there was quite a lot of damp mould and condensation around the skirting. This wasn't helped by the cupboard being there, but there was still plenty of ventilation and it shouldn't have been getting condensation. The infrared photograph shows that the temperature in that corner is 11°. My rule of thumb is that if something in the house is below 12° then there's a serious risk of condensation occurring at that point, and that's what we're seeing here.

Party Walls

These are the walls that divide one house from the next, for instance between two terraced houses and between the two houses in a pair of semis. In the case of a terraced house, this wall is most likely to be what we call a single brick wall, which is 225mm thick. It's reasonably well insulated for sound, particularly because the joists usually run from front to back, so the wall has no air paths between one house and the next. There can be problems around the staircase; this is not so much an issue with the staircase itself as with the trimmer that's built into the wall at either end of the staircase. These often shrink so that the mortar has gaps in it and, if these go right from one house to the next, noise can get through between the houses. If both houses are usually heated it doesn't really matter that the U-value of the wall between the two houses is not very good because the flow of heat from one house to the other, if they're both occupied, is approximately zero.

Most semi-detached houses were built after the introduction of the cavity wall. Although the early ones had 225mm solid walls between them, the majority have a cavity wall between the two houses. Sometimes this wall is solid when it gets to the loft. One of the ways that we try to find out what type of party wall construction was used is to go up into the loft and have a look. We've often been caught out, because there may be a solid 225mm wall in the loft, often with blocks laid flat, while the wall through the house itself is a cavity wall.

The building regulations used to maintain that a party wall should not be filled with anything – it must remain empty. Even when cavity wall insulation was installed, in the early days the party wall was not allowed to be filled with insulation. In the late 1980s or early 1990s, however, it was discovered that the party wall of a recently constructed three-storey building in the Midlands was very much colder than the outside walls of the house. This shouldn't really have been a big surprise because the party wall had no insulation in it, so there was nothing to stop outdoor air blowing around in that cavity, and that's what was happening.

I have called this type of issue an 'in-house winter cooling system', which is exactly what you do not want in a heated home, so it's very important to try and get rid of them all.

Consider an open cavity between a pair of semi-detached houses that has no filling of any kind in it and that probably runs right up through the loft to the underside of the roofing felt. If it changes to a solid wall above the first-floor ceiling, this makes it more difficult for wind to get in or out of it, as draughts would have to come in below ceiling level, that is from inside the eaves box or lower down through the wall.

This turns out to be a good thing because the warmer air in the cavity can't so easily get out so the party walls tend to be warmer. Even so, the house is going to be losing more heat through the party wall than through the outside walls once those are insulated, and we really want all the walls to be nice and warm because we're trying to live in the house.

Party walls from the mid-1970s onwards generally ran right up and finished roughly level with the top of the rafters. This was the case with the three-storey house mentioned above, whose party wall turned out to be colder than the outside walls. Because the cavity went right up to the underside of the roof and the block work there probably wasn't terribly neatly finished, it was possible for air to escape from the top of the wall. Convection currents inside the cavity could carry warm air up to the roof, and from there to the outside. Cold air could either fall down the cavity or enter near the bottom via the cavity all around the house below the damp course, from an under-floor void or through any hole, gap or crack that was joined to the party wall cavity. When it was windy, all these processes would combine to make the cavity and the blocks cold, and this is what was noticed.

A few years later, the building regulations changed, and cavity batts were built into party walls from then on. There are still plenty of homes that have party walls that are cooling both houses. We need to deal with this on a national scale, and I would say that filling all these with rockwool fibre would be a good plan.

Unusual Problems with Walls

Figs 8.22–8.24 here show some unusual patterns on an internal wall. We diagnosed this problem as being caused by slight dampening from condensation where the mortar lines of the blockwork were colder than the blocks themselves. This has caused the paint to go slightly darker exactly where every mortar line was in the blockwork; you can quite clearly see the rows of blocks and the bonds between

TOP LEFT, TOP RIGHT AND ABOVE: Figs 8.22–8.24 Condensation from mortar lines.

the blocks. This was a reversible process and only happened during very cold weather in this house. The residents didn't have cavity wall insulation, although they did get it shortly after our visit. The blocks were aerated concrete blocks and the cavities were very draughty.

Fig 8.25 shows another unusual problem, this time on the north side of a house. What we are seeing is mould growth where some of the blocks are gathering condensation as they get colder than others. Here again, we have aerated concrete block walls with uninsulated cavities. The mortar between the blocks is wicking heat out from the cavity, which is slightly warm because it is probably not as draughty as the one in the previous example.

There is no mould growing under the window, which is probably because the owners have a radiator under that window that warms the whole wall so much that condensation never forms on the outside of the wall where the radiator is. Heat flows around inside the cavity to warm the wall on each side of the window, just enough to keep the paint clear of mould. Above the window is cold and mouldy as little heat can get there from the cavity. The walls at the corners of the front part of the house are furthest from the heat source, but as heat rises it spreads sideways, explaining the pattern.

Fig 8.25 Mould growth on the front of a house.

Air Sealing Walls

Gaps at First-Floor Ceiling Level

We are going to start by looking up in a loft at the very edge of the ceiling (*see* also Chapter 12, The Downsides of Dot and Dab). In Fig 8.26 you can see over the edge joist and just get a glimpse of the top of the foil-backed plasterboard. Beyond that, the light grey is the edge of the wall lining board that comes up and stops just below the level of the ceiling. Beyond that is blockwork.

I quite like houses that are built using medium-density blocks. We used to call these breeze blocks; they have all sorts of different names now and they are far superior to aircrete blocks, which

Fig 8.26 Gap between the blockwork and wall lining.

Fig 8.27 The same wall after the gap was sealed.

were very popular from the 1980s through to the middle of the 2010s. I stopped using them in the 1990s because they cracked far too easily, both during and after construction. The tiniest amount of movement in the house, even slamming a door, could cause a block to crack; almost every house built from aerated concrete blocks has a hideous number of cracks – above every door, above every window, below every window and sometimes up in corners, as well as odd cracks in strange places. If the property had been wet plastered, even though it had cracked, the cracks could be repaired and the house would be reasonably airtight, at least in the rooms. When we moved over to dry lining instead of wet plastering, all these cracks disappeared behind the linings, letting in more draughts, which increased the heat loss of the house as it got older. This is not what we want.

Let's go back to Fig 8.26 and the loft with the breeze blocks that are visible beyond the edge of the plasterboard ceiling. It is not that easy to see, but there is a gap between the plasterboard and the blockwork. The gap was 10–15mm and was noticed by a conscientious homeowner during a very cold winter. He happened to go up in his loft and saw what seemed to be steam rising out from behind one of his walls; he almost thought it was smoke. He called me in to

investigate. I never saw the steam, but I did see the gaps and I advised him to fill them, because clearly warm air was rising behind his plasterboard linings and drawing heat away into his loft all the time during the heating season.

Fig 8.27 shows the same place but from a slightly different angle. You can now see that we have filled the gap with a fireproof foam to seal it. We also tidied up and replaced the insulation between the edge ceiling joist and the wall. This is missing in a lot of homes – you should go and check yours now. We added another layer of insulation at right angles to the joists, on top of everything, for good measure.

Redundant Air Bricks

These are the bane of a DraughtBuster's life. They are essentially holes that go from inside a home to outside and were intended in the 1950s and 60s to ventilate a bedroom or larder/cupboard. With the advent of domestic heating, air bricks were required to provide combustion air, most typically for open-vented gas boilers. We have written to both Corgi and GasSafe about this, suggesting to them that when such a boiler is removed then the air brick should either be removed also or blocked up if it is no longer needed. They have not taken any action, however, and thus thousands of homes have been left unnecessarily cold and draughty.

Old air vents in bedrooms are safe to block. The majority look like the one shown in Fig 8.28, which was in a bedroom cupboard. Stuffing the holes inside the room with tissue is the first action. The occupants have been very clever in making a DIY air sealing plate from a piece of plywood with Velcro on the back. As you can see, it can even be adjusted to change the air flow. As they had a window that they could open, we decided that we would leave it as it was, as they liked being able to ventilate the wardrobe.

Fig 8.29 is a Victorian cast iron vent, built into the wall of a bedroom. The vents shown in Figs 8.30 and 8.31 are probably from the 1950s, and again were built into bedrooms. These were mandatory for a while as it was thought that it was important to ventilate bedrooms, and these vents had to be permanently open. They should probably have been removed when central heating was installed because they were no longer needed.

Fig 8.28 Air vent in bedroom cupboard with a homemade sealing plate.

Fig 8.29 A Victorian vent that should have been sealed up or removed long ago.

Fig 8.30 Another old vent.

The vent in Fig 8.31 has been covered over with cling film and aluminium foil; it was obviously giving the owners a problem with draughts. If you have these types of ventilators, next time you decorate it's a good idea to remove them from the wall and fill the cavity with fibreglass, then fill the hole with aerated concrete block and plaster over it. We have seen people completely fill them with expanding foam and then plaster over that, but it does leave the wall a little prone to damage because the foam is not a sufficiently strong backing for finish plaster or filler.

Fig 8.31 A 1960s-style ventilator covered with foil and cling film.

Here are some examples of gaps around pipes. Fig 8.32 shows where a plumber installed a new bathroom in a Victorian house – probably about thirty years ago, as it had a cast iron bath. He never filled in around the hole, which was big enough to let in vermin, never mind draughts. The draught came in under the bath, from where it could get under the floor and out by the bath panel; this bathroom was very cold. DraughtBusters went back and filled around that pipe with some sand cement mortar, which imitated the pebble dash.

Fig 8.33 shows a washing machine pipe that's been bashed through a wall, while Fig 8.34 shows a similar pipe on the outside of the house. It is important to seal around pipes both internally and externally. There's one exception and that is gas pipes (Fig 8.35), where you should seal around the duct internally and externally, and between the gas pipe and duct

Fig 8.32 Hole around a narrow pipe going into a bathroom.

Fig 8.33 Washing machine pipe.

RIGHT: Fig 8.34 Washing machine pipe seen from the outside.

internally only. This is so that, were the gas pipe to leak, any gas would escape to the outside only.

Under the Bath

We encountered the situation in Fig 8.36 under a bath in 2020 – daylight was visible right round the pipe, and it was plumbed in only twenty years ago! The space above was big enough for birds, bats and other vermin to get in, and even wind-driven snow.

Please don't think that you are fine if you have an internal soil and vent pipe. The space under your bath will inevitably be connected to the soil pipe boxing and this in turn will be open right through

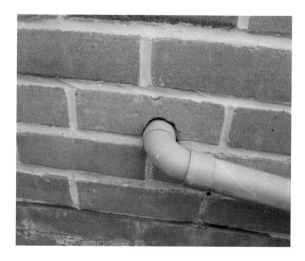

Fig 8.35 The 38mm waste pipe hasn't been sealed to the brickwork. This is slightly indicative of it not having been sealed internally either: waste pipes should be sealed round both internally and externally.

Fig 8.36 What is going on under your bath?

your house, including into the first-floor void and loft. Sadly, cold draughts can blow down through it or warm air can be drawn up and out of it. In either case, the result is heat loss, a cold bath(room) and discomfort if draughts are blowing in, not to mention the accompanying higher-than-necessary heating bills.

We also have lots of troubles in under-stair cupboards and meter cupboards. There are always loads of gaps, holes around where services enter, broken and missing floorboards, holes where old wires or pipes have been removed or meters changed – the list goes on. Have a look in your services cupboard, under your sink or anywhere where services enter your property.

Boiler Flues

This next problem is a bit trickier. We have a lot of trouble with boiler flues. Nearly all modern boilers have fanned flues, where the flue pipe is made up of two pipes, one inside the other, in a concentric formation. Most of these go out through a wall, and plumbers and heating engineers now use a diamond

drill to make the hole. This is always slightly bigger than it needs to be and is covered indoors and outdoors with a rubber bezel, which hides the fact that there is a gap between the flue and the wall. This gap is nearly always draughty. Sometimes the internal bezel is missing altogether and occasionally the outside one is missing, especially if it's high up.

The outer of these two pipes is always the one that draws in cold air from outside, for combustion purposes, so it's never going to get hot, which is why a rubber bezel can be used to cover up the gap. When we're draughtproofing, we always take a good look at the internal bezel to make sure that it's doing some good. If it's not, we pull it back slightly and have a look behind to see what kind of mess there is, and inevitably we must decide what to use to fill that gap with. With volunteers I don't particularly like using a foam gun, but that would probably be the best solution to this problem. Otherwise, we tend to use fibreglass or rockwool wedged into the gaps and fill or seal on top of that with plastic bags. Once the space is fully draughtproof, the bezel can be pressed back into place. Small gaps can be filled using acrylic sealant.

Fig 8.37 Boiler pipe going out through the wall.

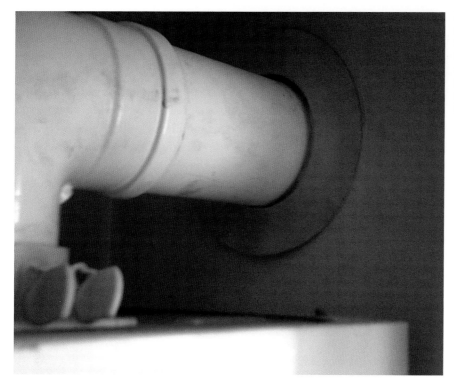

Fig 8.38 I don't even want to show you what was behind the bezel on this boiler but suffice it to say there are a lot of draughts coming in both between the bezel and the pipe and between the wall and the bezel.

We also check to see where the expansion pipe and condensation drain go, as these usually go to the outside through a hole that's been drilled by the fitter. We seal round these pipes both internally and externally.

Toilet Overflow Pipes

Nowadays, nearly all toilets have internal overflows, so it's only really in older homes that we encounter overflow pipes. Usually these don't have much of a draught around them, but we always check them and seal them internally with acrylic sealant. A bigger problem with overflow pipes is that wind can blow through the overflow pipe back into the toilet cistern. This might seem a bit extreme, but we worry about it and how to deal with it. Sometimes we find that a tee has been fitted to the outdoor end of the overflow pipe in an attempt to stop wind blowing back down it. The answer is probably to change it to an internal overflow if it's really causing an issue.

How Much Insulation?

We have talked quite a lot about cavity wall insulation, both about building it in and retrofitting it. You have seen that I built 300mm of insulation into my walls; I don't consider 50mm or 60mm of insulation anything like sufficient, so no matter what type of wall you have I would recommend that you have several hundred millimetres of insulation between you and the outside world. If you've got cavity walls then fill them. That is a relatively cheap and easy thing to do; following that, or if you've already done it, adding external wall insulation is the way forward. Many places in Europe commonly install 200mm of external wall insulation. It's true that it's not easy to do and may involve some work to the gable wall, extending the roof, or even, if the eaves don't poke out very far, extending them as well, but all these things are possible. As a bare minimum, I like to see 100mm of wall insulation; 200mm would be much better.

Which Type of Insulation?

I'm a great believer in reducing costs. To this end, I think we should design in the most economical form of insulation; I therefore suggest using fibreglass or mineral quilts or batts as your first choice for insulation as this works out as the cheapest option. For external wall insulation, I prefer to use things that can't possibly get wet, and this rules out any form of quilt or batts; for me, it also rules out all forms of organic insulation, including woodwool boards and so on.

As we also have to consider breathability, I come down on the side of expanded polystyrene. Extruded polystyrene and other forms of non-breathable insulation are more expensive than expanded polystyrene, although they do work out to be slightly thinner for the same insulation value. In central and northern Europe, the main product used for external wall insulation is expanded polystyrene; they have thicker sheets available there than we do. I prefer to use single sheets rather than multiple layers of thin sheets, so I'm hoping that our industry will start to provide 200mm, 250mm and 300mm thick sheets of expanded polystyrene in the near future.

Chapter Nine

Floors

Draughtproofing Floors

Many people live in homes with draughty floors. Typically, they are those with floorboards with gaps between the boards and with gaps under the skirtings. Don't assume this only happens on ground floors – it can happen upstairs, especially in houses with cavity walls!

We like using butyl rubber rolls made by DraughtEx. Their products are easy to use, quick to install and can be made to fit a range of gaps and cracks. These have proved very useful in draughtproofing suspended ground floors quickly and easily. Cheaper alternatives are string and wax, papier-mâché, masking tape or wood glue mixed with sawdust.

Suspended wooden ground floors are usually ventilated underneath, and this ventilation is important, as it helps to keep the timber in good condition. The downside is that outside air is blowing about

ABOVE LEFT, TOP RIGHT AND ABOVE RIGHT: Figs 9.1–9.3 Floorboards with gaps, cracks and holes.

underneath your floor, with only 20mm of wood between you and the outside world. You really don't want gaps between your floorboards, as then that wind can blow straight into your rooms and make them cold.

You may think that having a carpet would alleviate the problem. It does in most cases, but I can remember sitting in the lounge of the first house I bought and thinking that I was going mad because the carpet seemed to be rising and falling. It was a very windy day, and in time with the carpet rising and falling, the gas fire was repeatedly flickering, sometimes puffing out into the room and other times drawing too much. The carpet was acting like a massive bellows, pushing the air that we had just warmed with a gas fire up the chimney and sucking it in through all the gaps and cracks, under the door, around the windows, through socket outlets, under the skirting boards and the other places where draughts can come in, and cooling the room. The next day I took the carpet up and sealed all the gaps between the floorboards with masking tape. I also pushed rolled up newspapers under the skirtings. After that, the room was lovely and warm all the time and the carpet never bubbled up again.

Ideally, of course, all floors would be insulated as well as draughtproofed.

Skirtings

We often find gaps behind, under and in the corners of skirtings. The ones in Figs 9.4 and 9.5 are extreme cases – the skirtings were not even fixed! There was a slot for a wire, big gaps everywhere, and the edge of the floor was not sealed at all.

Figs 9.4 and 9.5 Skirting problems.

Fig 9.6 Gaps between skirting and floorboards.

of concrete in modern ones) and insulate the joists. Some people think that insulating between the joists is sufficient, but I much prefer to see sheet insulation under the joists – 50mm will just about do, 100mm is nice – then fibreglass or mineral wool will sit between the joists. Figs 9.7–9.14 show some work in progress.

No matter how much insulation you add under the floor, providing it is draughtproof, the effect will be that you instantly feel a lot warmer. The more insulation you add, the less the heat loss will be and the greater the savings you will derive.

When insulating a suspended wooden floor, the void will previously have been ventilated. It's very important that you keep this ventilation in place if there is still a void after the floor has been insulated.

Insulating Ground Floors

Wooden Floors

Suspended wooden floors are not easy to insulate. It is possible to overlay the floor with insulation and new flooring sheets, forming a new floating floor. The problem with this is that there is little point putting in 20mm or even 50mm of insulation when several hundred millimetres are required. Some insulation is better than none and the first thicknesses do good work, but in terms of future-proofing for sustainability, cost-effectiveness and simple logic, it is better to do the job well and properly the first time round, rather than having to redo it or retrofit more insulation later. The other downside of overlaying with an insulated floating floor is that all the door heights are reduced and the bottom riser on the stairs decreases.

The simplest way forward is to insulate from underneath by cutting and fitting insulation batts or quilt between the joists, and then ideally by underlaying the joists with sheet insulation; this will hold the insulation in place too. It's not always possible to work from underneath, as many floor voids are either inaccessible or too small to get into. In this case it is best to take the floor up, clean up the oversite (the ground beneath the floor – this is just dirt in old houses and a thin layer

Fig 9.7 Room ready for underfloor insulation to be fitted.

Fig 9.8 Part of the floor done.

Fig 9.9 The floor done under the wall.

Fig 9.10 Using membrane – I use strawberry netting.

Fig 9.11 A small area nearly completed.

Figs 9.12–9.14 Expanded polystyrene sheets used in the toilet to protect against the possibility of future leaks.

Fig 9.15 A typical Victorian air brick that helps to ventilate the underfloor void in a terraced house. Despite the spiders' activity, it has been kept nice and open; many are completely clogged with cobwebs, dust and dirt. Poking through a small bottle brush from time to time, combined with annual hoovering out, is the best way to keep them clear.

Completely Filling the Floor Void

Could we completely fill the void under a suspended wooden floor with insulation? Yes, it is possible and would be beneficial. But what about ventilation? If there is no void, then technically there is no longer a need for ventilation. This is the case with insulated ground-bearing slabs, where there is no void and no need for ventilation. I have extended this concept to include suspended wooden floors and have seen others completely fill the void with polystyrene beads, fifteen years ago, with no problems since.

For several years I've been trying to obtain grants to do trials of filling floor voids with polystyrene beads and have made many offers to help people do it in their homes. I did have an agreement with The Energy House, whereby we could go and fill the ground-floor void with polystyrene beads, carry out trials and test heat losses and energy use reduction, and then remove the beads afterwards, but we failed to get grant funding for this.

Recently I agreed to help a friend fill his floor void in a very cold extension with polystyrene beads (Figs 9.16–9.22). Fortunately, there were no wires or pipes in the void; it was very successfully filled

with polystyrene, and the extension is now warm and comfortable to live in.

We started by removing the kitchen island unit, along with laminate flooring boards and the floorboards themselves that were underneath it. Under the floor we found some noggins and fibreglass – likely draped over the noggins by the builders – and a polythene membrane covering the oversite. The bad news was that there was a gap between the fibreglass and the floor, so any intended insulation effect had been lost, as outdoor air could blow between the fibreglass and the floorboards, wicking away heat.

Fig 9.16 This hole is underneath the client's kitchen island.

ABOVE: Fig 9.18 Blowing beads to the ends and corners of the void using a bead blower gun powered by compressed air.

LEFT: Fig 9.17 Looking beneath the floorboards through the hole in the floor shown in Fig 9.16.

We opted instead to fill the whole floor void with polystyrene beads, although it was quite a fight to get them into the floor. Initially we used a compressor with a bead blower gun and a length of 28mm plastic pipe, but it was taking twenty minutes to empty a 10cu ft bag of beads into the floor void and it was sending them right to the end of the room. We found that a garden leaf blower worked extremely well but did make a little bit of a mess if anything went wrong; instead of sucking the beads into a collection bag we had to suck them from a box and then blow them out under the floor through a bespoke tube that we made for the purpose. In future we might well develop that setup a little bit more and have a 75mm flexible plastic pipe to direct them under the floor.

There are many potential objections to the idea of filling floor voids, including worries about fire, cables, gas pipes, radon, lack of ventilation, even the use of fossil fuels to make the insulation. These are discussed more fully below.

Fire Risk

It is very rare for a fire to break out in the floor void. Even if one did, every home should have smoke alarms fitted as standard, and these raise the alarm very quickly at the first sign of smoke.

Figs 9.19–9.21 Getting
the beads into the floor
space with a bead blower
gun was a fiddly job and
created a lot of mess.

Electric Cables

There is a physical reaction between expanded polystyrene and PVC cables. The polystyrene does slightly deplasticise PVC cables, but not to the extent of there being a problem. As the polystyrene absorbs the plasticiser, it shrinks back from the cable and has in any case insufficient mass to cause a serious issue. Hundreds of thousands of metres of electric cable are in contact with expanded polystyrene in many countries around the world without any trouble. No fires have been caused this way and there are no reports of cables becoming brittle.

Gas Pipes

Every time gas plumbing work is carried out, all the gas pipes are checked for leakage. Gas pipes don't usually leak, and when they do, we can smell it. Ultimately, it's no more of a problem to have a gas pipe under a floor than it is to have a gas pipe under a floor surrounded by insulation.

Fig 9.22 Filling the corners and edges of the underfloor void from outside using a 3m length of 22mm copper tube to help inject the beads. The edges of the floor void were already fully filled with beads and no more could be injected using this method, but it was a nice way to double-check.

Fig 9.23 The completed job before the floorboards were relaid. The mess of beads had been cleaned up using a dustpan and industrial hoover.

Radon

In areas where there are problems with radon, there are already measures in place to mitigate them. One of these could be ventilation under a floor void, and if this is the case then fully filling the void should not be done. It is possible to provide some forced ventilation by using a fan in an underfloor sump. All the regulations that relate to radon should still be followed for insulated floors.

Lack of Ventilation

The idea that moisture moves from the ground underneath a house into the house is a complete misconception – actually the reverse is true. Moisture in the form of water vapour is present in the air both inside and outside the house. We can measure the proportion of moisture in the air, and one of the measures used is called the partial vapour pressure of moisture in the air, which increases with the temperature of that air. Moisture moves from places where there is a higher partial vapour pressure to places where there is a lower partial vapour pressure; this is a very basic physical downhill process and is unstoppable by anything except a sheet of polythene or some other impenetrable material – that is, by separating the two volumes of air with an impermeable membrane. The partial vapour pressure of water vapour in the air is generally higher inside the house than outside or underneath it, so moisture moves from the house towards any places where the partial vapour pressure is lower.

When the floor void is filled with insulation, there is a temperature gradient through the insulating material between the rooms in the house and the cooler places under the house. So moisture in the air moves from the warmer air in the house down through the layers of insulation and into the ground under the house or out through the walls of the substructure and into the surrounding soil or surrounding air. This process does not involve air moving, only water vapour through the air. In very cold weather it may condense, but this condensation will occur on the very outside surface of the wall.

I have carried out some very simple experiments by putting polystyrene beads in a box in a tray of water with temperature and humidity sensors at various points in the layers of insulation. The movement of moisture is always away from the warmth in the test room down through the insulation and into the tray of water. This may seem counterintuitive, but it is a very basic physical principle and explains why my basement doesn't need water-proofing or tanking and why I've been living in that house for the last ten years with no damp mould or condensation.

Solid Floors

It may seem impossible to insulate solid floors but there are several methods of doing this. The most radical is to break up the screed and concrete down to the level of the oversite hardcore, then to carefully remove some of this, re-levelling and compacting what remains. It will then be possible to add sheet insulation, ideally 200mm of expanded polystyrene, a damp-proof membrane and new concrete and screed. This is only really viable if major renovation works are being carried out on the property.

An alternative method of insulating solid floors is to add 'wing insulation'. To do this, dig narrow trenches around the house, probably in sections, and then slide polystyrene down against the house wall into each trench so that it's touching the house; the trench can then simply be backfilled. The poly-styrene should go all the way down to the top of the footing, which in many cases will be between 600mm and a metre deep. It has been shown in New Zealand that, providing water isn't flowing through the insulation, the fact that it is wet makes almost no difference to the thermal conductivity and hence heat loss.

The effect of doing this is to reduce the amount of heat lost from beneath the building by warming up the soil and making the path length for heat to escape much longer. Most of the heat lost from a ground-floor slab is lost from the perimeter. This type of wing insulation effectively turns the soil underneath a house and below the level of the floor into additional insulation – not very good insulation, but more of it, nonetheless.

It is also possible to add wing insulation horizontally, just below the surface of the ground, say 300mm below, and ideally vertical insulation from there upwards to immediately below the damp-proof course. Again, this greatly increases the length of the path for heat to escape from under the building and so stabilises the temperature of the soil below the house, increasing comfort in the house and decreasing heat losses.

Suspended Concrete Floors

We have successfully insulated precast concrete plank floors by accessing the crawl space and adher-ing expanded polystyrene sheets to the underside of the planks. The insulation is inspected and any rectifications carried out every five years. Some sheets were removed following drainage and IT cabling works. On inspection, the missing ones were replaced and the undercroft generally tidied up. The client was able to recover the fee for the inspection through lower heat losses and bills in the following years.

Suspended Reinforced Concrete Floors

These can be insulated in a similar fashion, but you may encounter access problems, as voids can be var-iable in size – small or almost non-existent. Such voids can be filled with EPS beads, radon and ground gases permitting.

Beam and Block Floors

These have become very popular with developers following claims based on ground-bearing slabs that had sunk due to poorly compacted hardcore, which was often not done in layers and sometimes not to a suitable depth. Sadly, the majority of these will have tiny crawl spaces, often too low to access and with no way to get between bays. There are robots that can spray foam insulation onto the underside of such floor systems, but these are unreliable and require a nice, clean level oversite under the beam

Fig 9.24 Slight darkening at edge of a carpet due to draught.

and block floor, a thing we can only dream about. The beams sit slightly lower than the blocks, compounding the problems.

For me, insulation is applied too thinly, so filling small voids with expanded polystyrene beads or LECA would be my preferred option. Ground conditions, especially in relation to rotting vegetation, ground or nearby landfill gases and smells, must be thoroughly investigated and any issues eliminated first. I have considered using inflatable sausage balloons evenly spaced in deeper voids, and then filling over them with glued beads and popping the balloons, which would retain ventilation. This is all theoretical at present, but maybe more advanced robots will solve the problems for us in the future.

We also encountered a very surprising problem with one beam and block floor (Fig 9.24) in the hallway of a home with a beam and block floor and wooden stud partitions. Note the darkening to the edge of the carpet due to dust and dirt from outside, brought in by draughts, in this case through a beam and block ground floor that was not properly grouted.

What we think happened was that when the builders laid the floor, they left grouting it until later, knowing that the floor screeders would use a slurry of sand and cement to help them screed and to clean the floor of dust before they applied the screed. But before this happened, the ground-floor stud walls were constructed and so underneath the stud there were ungrouted blocks with gaps and draughts between them. Wiring and plastering were carried out and then the floor screed was done. They did do a slurry on the floor, but it didn't go underneath the floor plate, and then the plate shrank a tiny bit, leaving a gap between the screed and the timber of the stud wall. A draught could now enter through the beam and block floor, up the side of the soleplate and come under the skirting next to the carpet, producing this darkening at the edge of the carpet. In this case, it was also allowing cold air to blow in underneath the radiator, which was trying to heat the house. We also see this type of problem at first-floor level. On the ground floor, the solution is to take up the carpet and caulk the gap between the edge of the floor and the wall/skirting.

First Floors

It might come as quite a shock that a lot of the problems that we've talked about already can, but not necessarily do, apply to first floors as well. Chapter 13 covers first-floor voids in more detail. For now, we are just considering what happens where a floor joist is built into a cavity wall. When it is first built in, it has not fully dried out, so it shrinks a bit during the first few years; this leaves tiny gaps down each side of the joist where the blockwork used to touch it, and a slightly larger gap above the joist as it shrinks more in height (having more wood available to shrink in that direction).

A draught is quite common at that point, which is level with the bottom of the floorboard, the draught coming out underneath the skirting board. Sometimes you will notice this most easily if there is a light-coloured carpet in the room and the edges start darkening. This indicates that a draught is coming in. As it enters, it brings with it a certain amount of dust and dirt suspended in the air and this is effectively filtered out by the fibres of the carpet as it passes them, leaving the dark staining.

There can be other problems where draughts come in very easily. If there is a bay window, especially one that is tile hung, draughts are incredibly common. We have even seen cases where there is a bay window at both the front and back of the house and if you take the tiles off, you can see all the way through the house from the front to the back. There is no insulation, no draughtproofing, no air sealing whatsoever, just a howling gale blowing through underneath the floor. Those type of houses were typically constructed in middle of the last century and we do a bit better now, but there are still draughts in the first-floor void to watch out for even in newly built homes.

Where there is a lean-to roof abutting the house at ground-floor level, there can be lots of opportunities for draughts, especially if floor joists and roof joists are both built into the cavity wall and have left gaps in both the inside and the outside skin. These don't necessarily need to line up, but if they are in reasonably

Fig 9.25 Evidence of draughts entering between floor and skirting.

close proximity a draught can come from the roof, through the cavity and into the first-floor void, bringing with it cold air or letting warmed air out.

Having cavity wall insulation won't necessarily prevent these problems – it very much depends on the type of cavity insulation that you have. If you have old pumped-in white foam insulation, typical of the 1980s, then you might be okay, although this foam does tend to crack a bit like dried mud and the cracks can transfer draughts. But the problems won't be nearly so bad as if you have any form of sheet insulation in the cavity. Whether it's a partial fill or a full fill with sheet insulation, the wind just blows around the sheets as if they weren't there.

Built-in cavity batts, which you might think would stop most of the air blowing around, are usually installed badly, pulled apart, folded over, not quite the right size, and with gaps where they sit around wall ties or where they sit on top of wall ties and don't sit properly on top of the one below.

Worse than this is the fact that the bricklayers found it difficult to build cavity batts in. For example, for a 50mm cavity, the bricklayers would open that up to 60mm or 65mm to make it easy to lay the bricks and blocks without the cavity batts pressing on them. As a result, there may well be a gap between the cavity batt and either the bricks or the blocks or both, so wind can blow around them almost as badly as it does with sheet insulation. Add to this the fact that the batts themselves aren't windproof and air can move through them, and you can see that there's always going to be a problem with wind blowing about in the cavity.

If you have blown fibres, then air can pass through them very easily; it can even blow them around.

They tend to settle a little bit and there are often lots of voids.

In short, there's no guarantee that wind won't be blowing around in the cavity with almost all forms of cavity wall insulation. Have a look at the big gap between the two blocks in Fig 9.26, where you can see the bricks of the outside skin. This house had cavity walls insulated with built-in batts, but there is no sign of them through this gap.

The new generation of cavity foams are a lot better. We haven't really had time to find out how well they perform or how well they are installed, but I suspect they will be much better in terms of preventing wind blowing around in the cavity and getting into the first-floor void as they don't shrink as they age like the older PU foams did.

Fig 9.26 Gap between blocks in the first-floor void. Also note the missing insulation, evidenced by the fact that we can see the bricks and mortar of the outside skin through the gap.

Chapter Ten

Doors and Windows

Doors

The Front Door

There may be draughts through or round the panels in all doors and all doors can warp. The front door shown in Figs 10.1 and 10.2 exhibits several problems.

The door is a cottage-style door, smaller than normal, which is a good thing, as smaller = less heat loss and fewer potential draughts. It has a cat flap, which isn't ideal, but this one didn't seem to be draughty.

So far so good. Looking at the bottom of the door in Fig 10.3, the right-hand side of the door frame has rotted, falling away so much that we can see daylight. There's a nasty draught there. The brush strip across the bottom of the door is not ideal in the first place, but it doesn't touch where you can see daylight towards the left-hand side of the door. Our solution to this is to trim everywhere else on the draught strip with a very sharp pair of scissors, in this case probably 3mm everywhere except where the daylight is visible, and then refit the draught strip

Figs 10.1 and 10.2 Front door showing common problems.

Fig 10.3 Daylight coming in under the door frame where the wood has decayed.

BELOW LEFT: Fig 10.4 The door in Fig 10.1 opened.

BELOW RIGHT: Fig 10.5 Hinge side of door frame.

3mm lower. It is a labour of love but it's well worth doing. We much prefer to see a positive step on all thresholds which lead to outside, so that a good seal can be formed when closing the door.

Opening the door reveals further issues. The frame has factory-fitted draught strips, but compare how clean the frame and head are on the hinge side of the door (Fig 10.5) with the dusty and dirt visible on the other side (Fig 10.6). Fig 10.7 shows the dust and dirt increasing from left to right. The reason for this becomes clear once the door is closed again.

ABOVE: Fig 10.7 Top of the door frame.

LEFT: Fig 10.6 Head frame.

BELOW LEFT: Fig 10.8 Closed door with daylight visible through the crack.

BELOW RIGHT: Fig 10.9 Pressing on the door narrows the gap so no daylight is visible.

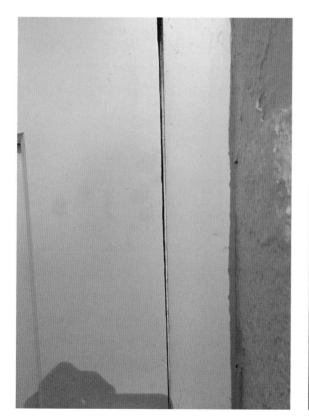

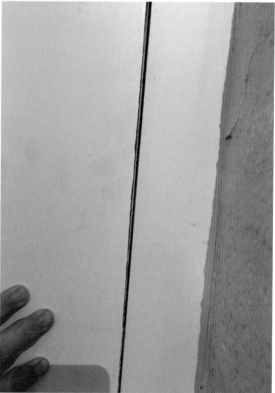

It is possible to see daylight in the crack when the door is shut, but when we press on the door, the daylight disappears. This is because the latch is not securely holding the door against the draught strips but is letting in light and draughts. All that is needed to resolve the problem is for the lock keep to be moved 4mm to bring the door tight onto the draught strip when closed. This leads to no daylight being visible and no draughts. The door should not be able to wobble when shut and locked. Note that if you move a striker plate or keep you will need to check that any deadlock is still functioning correctly, as its keep may need to be moved over too.

You may have noticed there is no threshold strip but only a draught brush. These are all right when it is not very windy, but I always prefer to see a threshold with a step in it or a weather bar that positively touches the door with some form of compressible strip – anything that has positive contact. Generally, inward-opening doors have a rebate at the bottom and a weather bar in the sill or threshold.

If your door does not have draught strips you can fit them. Figs 10.10 and 10.11 show a door before and after adding a draught strip.

On the hinge side, the strip should be adhered to the face that the hinges have been cut into. On

Fig 10.10 Hinge side of a door.

Fig 10.11 Hinge side of the same door with a draught strip.

the latch side and head, the strip should be fitted onto the side of the door stop. This is so that they are compressed as the door closes. On the head, use the same face as the latch side, wrapping round the corner to join the one on the hinge side.

When shut, the door should not wobble. Care needs to be taken to select the correct style and thickness of draught strip. Styles range from thin cheap foam to the butyl rubber ones used here, or brush pile. Wedge-shaped ones are also available; these fit into the corner between the door frame and door stop sections of the frame.

Thicknesses can go from 1mm up to 6mm or 8mm jumbo foam rolls. For gaps thinner than 1mm, apply

ABOVE: Fig 10.13 Draught strip on the head, joining up with the one on the hinge side.

LEFT: Fig 10.12 Draught strip fitted on the latch side of a door.

BELOW LEFT AND BELOW RIGHT: Figs 10.14 and 10.15 Butyl rubber draught strips. I normally use white draught strips on white frames but have used brown in these examples for clarity.

oil or Vaseline to the door and a neat thin bead of silicone to the frame, close the door and leave it closed for several hours. On opening, the sealant will have perfectly taken the shape necessary to seal the gaps and the oil or Vaseline can be cleaned off; it was only there to prevent the sealant sticking to both surfaces. The edges of the sealant can be tidied up with a sharp knife if necessary.

Letterplates

These can be very draughty and may even blow open and flap in high winds. Sometimes when mail is pushed through, it remains in the opening, leaving both flaps partly open and allowing draughts to blow into the house all day. We fit a lot of letterplate draughtproof inner flaps, always containing brushes,

ABOVE LEFT: Fig 10.16 Front door with daylight showing around the frame. Daylight being visible means it will be draughty, but this is easily fixed with draught strips, either self-adhesive or pinned-on ones with plastic or aluminium carriers.

ABOVE RIGHT: Fig 10.17 The outside of the door in Fig 10.16. It would be very easy to add a porch door to this front door. Benefits would include lower heat losses from walls and down through the porch ceiling, which is almost certainly not insulated. You can see that this house had a porch door once.

Fig 10.18 Daylight, draughts and snow can come in through this one!

RIGHT: Fig 10.19 There's too much daylight visible here too. The lock keep could be adjusted or draught strips added, or both.

BELOW RIGHT: Fig 10.20 Letterplate flap inner draught seals; one has a secondary flap.

and sometimes with a flap as well. These are simple to install, often involving just four screws, and they do a wonderful job.

There are alternatives. The Letterplate Eco's draughtproofing is integrated in the design and the neat offset cuts mean it is held firmly shut against its frame, no matter which direction air flow comes from. It's designed to let post through easily while stopping draughts. This is achieved by using a balanced flap that opens effortlessly but closes firmly behind itself every time, whether there is no air flow, low air flow or high winds, meaning no further draughtproofing is necessary. As it uses its own balanced weight to close, it won't pinch fingers or chew post.

Most other letterbox draught excluders form a physical barrier to the elements, usually brushes or flaps, but these also form a barrier to postal deliveries. They are normally held in place by springs or hinges that can rust and break, but the Letterplate Eco won't do that.

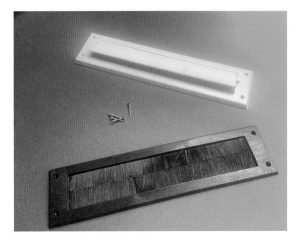

The Eco is available with or without trunking to suit new doors or old, and can be composite or wooden.

On my own house I decided not to have a letterplate in my front door as the potential for draughts and unwanted heat losses was too great in a home with no heating system. Instead, I installed a wall-hung stainless steel letterbox in my porch.

Figs 10.21 and 10.22 The Eco flap is a cleverly balanced inner letterplate cove that can't be blown open by the wind.

The Back Door

The back door in Fig 10.24 is typical of many wooden back doors. The door has warped and is only held closed by a single lock and latch at the height of the mid rail. It is quite clear that there is a significant gap between the door and frame, and this is evident by the daylight that's coming in through the gap; there will be draughts coming in through that gap too. During their visit, DraughtBusters fitted self-adhesive draught strips to this door, which only took about ten minutes and completely cured the problem.

UPVC Doors

It might be tempting to think that uPVC doors are not draughty, but this is unfortunately not the case. In recent years we have come across quite a few uPVC doors that have warped to such an extent that their

Fig 10.23 Outside letterbox.

RIGHT: Fig 10.24 Back door with daylight and draughts.

rubber draught seals are no longer making contact with the door(s) and a draught is consequently entering at these places. It's worth checking all round all your doors with the back of your hand to see whether a cold draught is coming in between the frame and the door itself. We also find that the doors sometimes don't close tightly against the seals. There are usually adjusters on the keeps, not just for the latch and the lock but also for the multipoint locking systems. Simply adjusting these can bring the draught strips back into contact. Sometimes, especially at the bottom of the door, the draught strip has been damaged or gone missing; it may be lying around nearby but in many cases it has disappeared altogether. Fortunately, on most uPVC doors there are two draught strips, one on the frame and one on the door, which close together to form a draught seal. It is better to have both in place and functioning than to have just one.

There can be problems with draughts entering round the frames, so you should check to see if sealant is present round the outside of the door frame. Usually it is, but sometimes there are small gaps where draughts can enter and get in behind the frame. If you have any gaps, these should be filled back in with new silicone of the same colour as used originally. Then check around the frame internally. There may well be a little crack between the frame and the wall, and we recommend sealing this using acrylic sealant or decorator's caulk.

Fig 10.25 Loose draught seal.

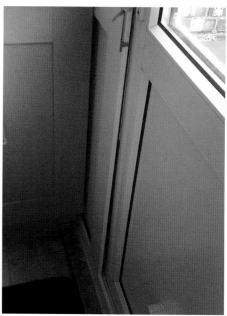

RIGHT: Fig 10.26 UPVC door with gap at bottom between the door and the frame.

The other big problems that we encounter are underneath the sill. Go outside and have a look underneath your door sill or threshold and see if there is a gap under the frame. It may still be sitting on temporary packers with no attempt to fill the gap; ideally, it should be fully filled with mortar. If there is a gap, then a draught can blow in under the door and from there it can blow up both sides of the frame, which is why we like to see the frame sealed internally. A draught can also come out between the sill and the floor, so that gap needs sealing internally. Clear silicone is a good choice for that gap, even if there doesn't appear to be one.

Fig 10.27 A sill on packers with draughts entering underneath it.

French Double Doors

UPVC Double Doors

UPVC French doors are notorious for dropping and going out of square. The weight of the glass can deform the door. When doors are made, the glass needs be set squarely into the door surround using spacers, which I call 'heel and toe packers'; otherwise, when hung, the glazed doors 'drop' and go out of square, fouling on the threshold. The glazing holds the door frame square, so it is crucial that these spacers are correctly and tightly in place and that they are doing the job of keeping everything in place. If they are not, then the frame will slightly deform, with the hinge side staying up and the closing side moving down slightly, typically rubbing on the sill or threshold. Sometimes it rubs so badly that it becomes very difficult to open. If this happens to you, then try lifting the door; by taking a lot of the weight, you will probably be able to open it, but you will need to adjust it.

Even when the door has gone slightly out of square, it is usually possible to raise the hinges enough so that it still closes. Good hinges have several adjusters on them, and one of these allows you to lift the door with respect to the frame. Some of the other adjusters are a little bit more difficult to get at but allow you to pull the top of the door in towards the frame and or to push the bottom of the door away from the frame. Both of those actions will help to raise the closing side just a little bit.

You should look at the seals on the door frame and on the doors themselves to make sure that they are all still in place, as described above for single uPVC doors. If any are missing, then you should replace them with new ones. They usually press into a slot in the frame and are very easy to fit. The awkward thing is to find the right one. It is possible to buy a selection of rubber draught strips for uPVC windows and doors online and this will help you decide which one you need. Then you can buy a small roll and replace the draught strips yourself.

Wooden French Double Doors

All the same checks listed above for single doors need to be carried out on French double doors and frames. You can just follow the same process for them. French double doors are rarely final exit doors, and they don't really need handles on the outside. We find that many French doors don't close properly and rely on some form of bolt or security bolt to hold the slave leaf (the secondary side of the door that opens last) in place when closed. These are problematic: they don't hold the closed leaf in place properly; then when the primary opening leaf closes, it doesn't hit its draught seals because the other leaf isn't closed.

Our recommendation for all French wooden double doors is to use an espagnolette lock. This type of lock simultaneously operates a shoot bolt at the top and the bottom with a single handle in the middle, which can be used to pull both doors tightly closed onto all the draught strips and secure them. The major advantage of this type of lock is that there is no handle on it on the outside, so it's completely secure when closed. These are common on the continent but rarely used in the UK. There are also some available that can be positively locked.

Fig 10.28 Daylight and draughts coming through a French door.

If the existing locking arrangements work without letting in draughts, then they can remain in place. Most often, some additional draught strips or adjustment will be needed.

Patio Doors

A standard set of sliding patio doors has one fixed leaf and another that slides across it on rollers. The rollers should be oiled regularly with silicone oil. You should use a can with a lance on it and squirt oil through the adjustment hole at the end of the bottom member of the patio door frame. It doesn't need a lot of oil – just one small squirt on each side annually will be perfect and will keep the roller lubricated. The track should be cleaned regularly too.

The next thing we look for is draughts around the frame, as described above for other doors. Follow through the process of looking under the frame and sealing it inside and out and across the bottom.

We check all the draught strips on patio doors. Normally these are brush pile, and they fit into slots in the frame and door sections and can slide up or down. Ensure that brush strips are present for the full length of any frame or door member. They sometimes move and break off, leaving parts of the draughtproofing missing. The one on the threshold can even disappear altogether, so you should check that it is there. The brush strips are keeping chilly air out of the home in the winter, so and you need them all present.

There should be no draughts at all around the fixed leaf and it should not be able to move. The sliding leaf should be closed to within 5mm of the lock side style, and you should look to see if it is parallel with this jamb. It usually will be, but sometimes it may have gone out of parallel; this creates a small problem on the lock side, but a bigger problem at the meeting style, potentially to such an extent that the draught strips aren't engaging and there's a draught in the middle of the patio door. The door can be adjusted by lifting it a little with a lever bit and using

a screwdriver through the holes described above where oil is squirted in. You should make sure there's no weight on the rollers when you're trying to adjust them, as it's very easy to strip the threads or mash the head of the screw or bolt that turns the threads.

Once you get everything parallel, check to see that it all rolls freely backwards and forwards and that the locks all still work.

Wooden patio doors may need a special clip halfway up the meeting style to pull the outer leaf inwards and tightly onto the inner leaf so that draughts don't come in and ensure that all the draught strips are engaging. Suitable clips can be obtained from an ironmongery supplier.

Sliding folding doors (bifolds) are much more difficult and have far more potential problems. People who own these can probably afford to get specialists in to sort them out if necessary, and this is what we suggest.

Pet Doors and Cat Flaps

You will have noticed that the back door in Fig 10.24 had a cat flap. Cat flaps have a very poor record in the world of DraughtBusters. Almost every one we've ever seen has been letting in draughts, not just through the flap itself but around the flap, around the frame and through the frame of the flap. They are often made of cheap plastic and are not very durable. They are also difficult to seal up, but it's definitely worth doing this if there's no longer a pet living at the property. With the permission of the owner, we use silicone on the outside and acrylic sealant on the inside and we ensure that there are absolutely no draughts left. We recommend removing cat flaps altogether, but that obviously leaves a hole in the door and that's not very easy to repair. For some doors, new panels can be purchased or additional panels affixed to the inside and outside of the door. The new innovative 'Petflaps', as shown in Fig 10.29, may be of interest to some; they are draughtproof and can't blow open (www.thepetflap.com).

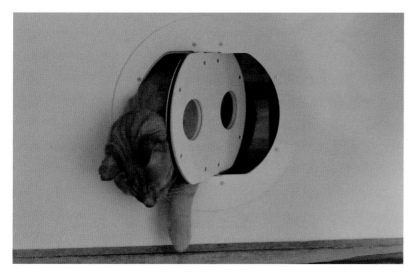

Fig 10.29 The Petflap – an improvement on the standard cat flap.

BELOW LEFT AND BELOW RIGHT: Figs 10.30 and 10.31 This window, even though it had been lived with for thirty years, had daylight showing between the sash and frame (in the near bottom left corner of the opening casement). We moved the friction stay hinge over 5mm to the left, and this resulted in there being no more draughts.

Internal Doors

We do not recommend draughtproofing internal doors except to cold areas. Always check that the doors latch, and that locks and deadlocks operate after any draught strips have been applied.

Windows

Start with a careful inspection, looking for cracks and gaps both around and through the frames, dark staining, cracks or gaps under sills or window boards, and draughty trickle ventilators.

Check that the window shuts against its frame or draught strip. There is a multiplicity of different types of sealing strips available and this is not a one-size-fits-all problem. We use small, medium and large rectangular foam strips, brush pile strips and E, P or D butyl rubber strips, all in brown or white. We also use nail or screw-on plastic carriers with brush-pile strips. We then seal the gaps in the frame or in

the glazing itself with silicone outside and acrylic sealant inside. You may use good-quality silicone inside between non-wood and non-plaster surfaces; otherwise using acrylic sealants is best.

Problems with Windows

The pictures here illustrate frequently encountered problems with windows.

Trickle Ventilators

Trickle ventilators are devices generally fitted at the top of a window that allow fresh air to circulate naturally through a room and help dissipate stale air. They are controllable, to give the option of having them open or closed.

During the 2021/2022 season we encountered a lot of problems with trickle ventilators. These can be draughty when closed, insect protection may be gone or decayed, they won't close, or the householder can't or doesn't know how to open them.

Draughtiness

We found that in a lot of cases draughts were emanating from the trickle vents even when closed. These vents were surprisingly insubstantial, and it was rather a shame to find that they were letting in draughts. It would be possible to seal them to the frames to prevent some of the draughts, but this would be tricky. If the windows can be used in a ventilated position – fixed in a secure vent position using the second position on the window keep – then we recommend sealing up the trickle ventilators.

Fig 10.32 The rubber glazing gasket has shrunk away from the corner. As uPVC frames have drained and ventilated glazing rebates, unwanted draughts will be entering. A careful touch of clear or black silicone will work but black looks better.

RIGHT: Fig 10.33 Here a replacement length of gasket is best.

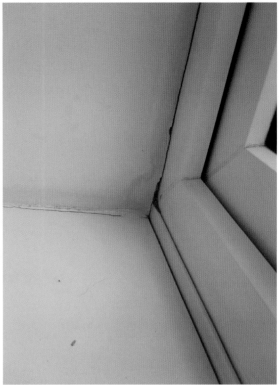

ABOVE LEFT: Fig 10.34 Either a touch of silicone or replacement gasket will work to fill this gap. As a temporary fix, a small piece of rolled up thin black polyethene will do the trick.

ABOVE RIGHT: Fig 10.35 Gaps between frame and wall should be caulked, as well as gaps along the sill. We often prefer to use white silicone on UPVC or aluminium windows in this situation.

Fig 10.36 Sealant not touching the window. Simply reapply silicone sealant around the window frame and check under the sill.

Fig 10.37 This window sill has been sealed underneath using clear silicone, but many are not sealed.

Fig 10.38 This bathroom window is not closing at the top on the hinge side, as the friction stay is no longer hooking into the end retainer, a piece that is often made of plastic. These can be replaced but there are lots of variations to watch out for: length, fire opener, stacking height (how big the stay is when closed), position of screws. Finding an identical friction stay obviously makes replacement easier.

RIGHT: Fig 10.39 This window didn't close on the hinge side. Again, it is best to fit a pair of new friction stays.

ABOVE: Fig 10.41 An older wooden window with draughty gaps between the plaster and the frame. Simply caulk this gap. Also check outside and seal the frame to the wall outside. With painted windows it is better to use frame sealant rather than silicone, as silicone generally can't be painted over.

LEFT: Fig 10.40 Another window that didn't close properly. The problem is becoming very common, leaving many double-glazed windows draughty up the hinge side.

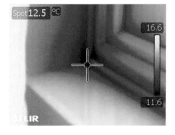

Fig 10.42 Thermal image of a lounge window with cold draughts entering between the window and window board. The window had been replaced and not properly sealed. The cold in the bottom corner is common but here it was compounded by excessive thermal bridging due to missing cavity wall insulation. When rectified under guarantee, this corner was no longer cold enough to cause problems with condensation. The draughts were sealed using caulk.

Missing Insect Protection

We have identified whole estates where trickle ventilators have lost their insect protection. The commonest problems are with over-the-head-type arrangements. The insect grilles become brittle and fall out or are knocked out with the window cleaner's brushes.

Problems Closing

This is a different issue from draughty when closed, as draughty ventilators do close, and a draught enters between the ventilator and the frame. Ventilators that don't fully close allow draughts all the time. Some ventilators have plastic clips that hold the closing piece in place, and these can come adrift or break, and the vent then remains open all the time.

There are many different types of trickle ventilators, and there are many and varied ways of opening them. Some push to the left or right, some up or down, others click open, while others need a sharp

Figs 10.43 A trickle ventilator with missing insect guarding.

Fig 10.44 Ventilator in the closed position, shown from the inside.

Fig 10.45 The same ventilator open; it is often possible to half open trickle ventilators.

but gentle press. It is not surprising that some people can't open them. The ones in Fig 10.46 slide sideways and, once slid open, they can tilt to direct draughts up or down.

We often have to explain to householders how to open and close their trickle ventilators. They could ask their neighbours or have a search online. Usually just having a go is a good way to find out how to open them, and closing them is usually the opposite operation. In general, it's best to keep them closed and use them only when needed; we prefer to open windows when ventilation is needed.

The ventilators in Fig 10.48 are tricky to operate unless you're familiar with them. A gentle but sharp jab on the grey symbol opens them one end at a time and the same sharp press is used to close them.

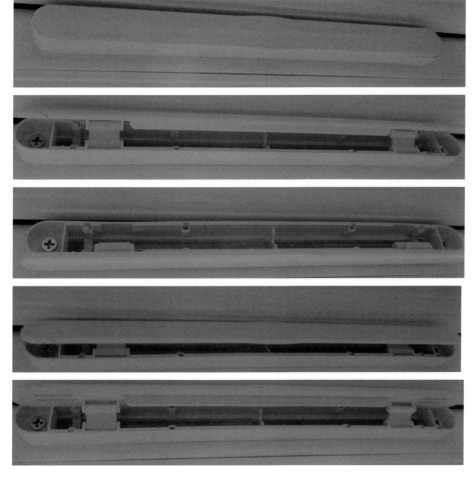

ABOVE LEFT: Fig 10.46 Ventilator with sliding opening mechanism.

Fig 10.47 Top to bottom: trickle ventilator closed; partly open; fully open but with flap pulled downwards; one-third open; and fully open with flap pushed up.

Fig 10.48 Push-to-open ventilators. Left to right: fully closed; open at the bottom; open at the top; fully open.

Trickle ventilators are another bane of a Draught-Buster's life. They were intended to allow draughts in in a controlled way but are proving themselves to be unfit for purpose. We see ventilation as an active thing, to be controlled by occupants as and when required. A general government directive of 'one size fits all' has resulted in draughty homes. We have said before that draughts do too much by way of ventilation when it is windy and not enough when it is calm. Trickle ventilators should now be outlawed in the interests of saving energy. Controllable ventilation is what is needed.

A paper has been published that shows that trickle ventilators only work when the door to the room is left open. An interesting graph from that article analysing why people don't use trickle ventilators can be seen at www.mdpi.com/ijerph/ijerph-12-08480/article_deploy/html/images/ijerph-12-08480-g001.png.

Window Ironmongery

Older windows, especially wooden casements, have only one place where the window handle closes them. This usually isn't a problem, although it can be, especially for larger casements. Early replacement windows used cockspur handles, which frequently only closed at one place or had one handle for each sash. We very much approve of the new style of multipoint locking handles, where the handle operates a rail to shoot bolts across so that the window is closed in several places at once. These also give the option of a fixed secure ventilation position.

Draught Strips

There is a very useful tip that will help you to check whether your draught strips are working or not that

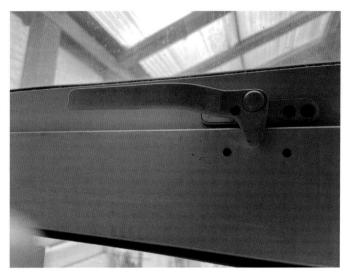

ABOVE: Fig 10.50 A cockspur handle with a missing wedge piece, which leaves this double-glazed draught-stripped window draughty when closed.

LEFT: Fig 10.49 Multipoint window handles.

involves shutting a piece of paper into the window and trying to pull it out (*see* Chapter 5, Checking Windows for Draughts box). If it pulls free very easily then the chances are that the draught strip isn't touching the frame properly and needs to be replaced, or the window needs adjusting.

Doors can generally be adjusted but windows rarely, and increasingly we're coming across uPVC windows where the seals have ossified, are no longer squashy and hang back slightly from the frame, allowing draughts to come in. It's relatively easy to replace these as a DIY project; there are universal strips available and we find that they work very well. Sometimes it's more difficult to get the old ones out than to get the new ones in. A bit of soapy water will help to fit the new ones but when they are brittle it's nearly always a job for a Stanley knife to get the old ones out; great care needs to be taken when working using sharp tools.

We are also finding that some of the lower-quality uPVC windows are warped up the hinge side of the casements. On the better-quality windows there are two wedges that help to bring the middle of the sash in towards the frame as it closes. These can also be obtained and retrofitted, although it is not always easy to get them in the perfect position so that they hold the inside style tightly against its draught strip.

Metal Casement Windows

Metal casement windows have troubled us for a long time. The window casements and top-hung lights tend to warp and deform, giving rise to draughts through awkward small and slightly tapering cracks. These are unsuitable for draught strips, and have been instead professionally remedied by specialist companies using silicone sealants applied to the frame and a release agent to the casements.

We have followed this same process for one client. It is crucial that the frame is perfectly clean and free of all dust and flaking paint before starting. Then we applied a liberal film of Vaseline to the sash and the silicone to the frame. On closing the window, the silicone forms a perfect seal, filling all the gaps, whatever their size or shape. Once cured – typically after four or five hours, depending on the thickness, the type of silicone and the humidity – the window can be opened; the Vaseline must then be cleaned off both surfaces with an absorbent cloth, after which the window frame should be washed with detergent and water a couple of times, then wiped clean with water. Any excess sealant that may have squidged out can be carefully cut away with a sharp knife. It is better to carefully tool the silicone back to the frame on closing the window, but it must not touch any exposed surfaces that have not been Vaselined.

The results were instantly appreciated by the occupants. The room was noticeably quieter and draught-free, which meant it was warmer in winter and cooler in summer, with less energy required for air cooling or heating. A serendipitous and remarkable additional benefit is that the occupants are seeing far fewer insects than previously, presumably because they can't get in through the cracks that have been sealed up.

Sliding Sash Windows

For help with draughtproofing sliding sash windows, the Historic England website is a very useful resource (historicengland.org.uk). Don't forget to seal around the frame and architraves.

Sliding sash windows are generally in excellent condition because they are set back into the reveal and are surrounded by lime mortar that sucks moisture away. Draughty sash boxes help with reducing moisture, too (don't let those draughts into the house though). It's traditional and important to keep the sides of the side rails, and the underside of the bottom rail, unpainted. Both bottom rail and sill should slope downhill towards the outside in order to direct water away from the frames. It is also important that frames are made from top-quality dry seasoned wood. Chapter 14 explores sliding sash windows in more detail.

Roof Windows

Roof windows that are over twenty years old start to run into problems with their draught seals. These items are serviceable but almost no one services roof windows; they seem to be fitted and forgotten. The flashings need clearing and cleaning and dust filters replacing but, more importantly, the draught strip on the closing bar is subject to high temperatures and falls apart. These are simple to replace and readily available.

Insulating Windows

Windows can be improved in several ways so that they lose less heat. So far, we have only considered draughtproofing. Windows can also be double glazed, either by using a secondary glazing system, a simple sheet of cellophane, or by replacing the glass or even the whole frame with double glazing. Replacing a window is a major and expensive operation and sometimes disruptive to decoration, especially if the building is either rendered or painted on the outside.

The UK has an excellent infrastructure for replacing windows with new double-glazed ones. You can choose from wood, aluminium, plastic or even fibreglass frames, and you can also choose the type of glass that you have in your window. Low-E glass is a good choice; this is a special glass that has a film on it that reduces heat loss from inside the building. The effect is much the same as having the curtains drawn during the day but being able to see out of them as well. (Drawing the curtains will also make something like a 5 per cent saving in the heat loss from the room,

Figs 10.51–10.53 Decayed draught seals on roof windows.

and that is sufficient to make the room feel warmer almost instantly in the evenings.)

What most people don't realise is that low-E glass has the opposite effect in the summer, keeping the house cooler than if you just have ordinary double glazing. The most effective way to reduce overheating, however, is to shade the windows externally during the day in very hot weather and to open the windows at night wherever possible to let the heat escape.

The double-glazing industry is very loath to offer triple-glazed windows because the frames are not capable of carrying the extra weight of glass and the hinges tend to break. In central and northern Europe, triple glazing is now standard, and if you want double glazing you have to pay extra for it; for instance, if you wanted to have just a double-glazed window in your garage in Europe you probably wouldn't bother because it would cost you more to have that than to have the triple-glazed product.

Window Reveals in Dry-Lined Homes

It is important to properly insulate around windows. Traditionally, a lot of thermal bridges have routinely been built into our window details, for example, by using masonry to close the cavity at the reveal, or through metal lintels that extend from inside to outside. Furthermore, there is often no insulation under windows or even in the reveals, due to poor workmanship or incorrect installation.

ABOVE LEFT: Fig 10.54 A typical window reveal before we started. Note some damp marking to the bottom of the painted reveal. This is darker due to condensation, which in turn is due to the reveal being so cold.

ABOVE RIGHT: Fig 10.55 Taking a peek at the window reveal behind the reveal lining uncovered a multitude of sins.

ABOVE LEFT: Fig 10.56 The plasterboard fully removed from a window reveal. Note the presence of thermal bridging, made worse by the use of bricks (just visible next to the triangular plaster dob). Also note that there are lots of gaps between the masonry and the vertical dpc. Draughts could blow behind the reveal lining, on round the corner and behind the wall lining boards.

ABOVE RIGHT: Fig 10.57 Having almost finished cutting out the masonry, the reveal is ready for insulation and thermal lining.

LEFT: Fig 10.58 Insulation added in the cavity and foam applied to the edge of the wall lining board. It is also possible to use sheet insulation to close the cavity or a proprietary cavity closure. I prefer to use sheet insulation friction fitted and then sealed with foam or acrylic sealant to make it draughtproof before adding the reveal lining.

ABOVE LEFT: Fig 10.59 Thermal lining board added. This is a piece of composite plasterboard with insulation bonded to the back of it, fully adhered to the end of the blockwork with foam.

ABOVE RIGHT: Fig 10.60 A refinished reveal, ready to redecorate.

Fig 10.61 Carefully filling the space between the wall (note the use of thermally bridging bricks again) and the plasterboard with polystyrene beads. Tap the plasterboard to help the beads settle. This works many times better than foil radiator deflectors.

ABOVE LEFT: Fig 10.62 The void between the plasterboard and the blockwork under a window filled with insulating polystyrene beads.

ABOVE RIGHT: Fig 10.63 The top of the plasterboard below a window board has been filled with foam. The window board will be refitted by fully bedding it using fixing foam and sticking it to the window frame with acrylic sealant, leaving no paths for draughts to get in.

Draughts are frequently present under window boards, either emanating from the cavity or sometimes directly from outside. Coupled with this, frames that are not fully sealed to the masonry allow draughts to enter; these draughts can most easily be detected by paying attention to blackening of the cracks or dark shadowy streaks on the frames. We found a couple of extreme examples of draughts where it was possible to see straight over the window head from indoors, or straight out under the window board, across the top of the cavity and out under the outside windowsill into the garden! Always look for cracks and gaps first, then check with the back of your hand to feel for draughts. The ultimate search weapons are feathers, lit candles, infra-red thermometers and thermal imaging cameras.

The pictures here illustrate how to rectify window reveal and window board problems in homes that have been dry lined or that have cavities closed with masonry.

Insulation

Insulating Doors

We frequently come across doors that have plywood panels in the bottom of them, typically back doors. This plywood is usually only 6mm thick and so it has very little insulation value. If you have one like this then we recommend adding insulation on the inside by fitting a piece of foam-foil insulation board tightly into the panel (we suggest 20mm or 25mm thick, the

Fig 10.64 Sealing under a window board with caulk.

thicker the better), and then fitting another panel of plywood over the top of it and some wooden trims round it.

Many doors have wooden panels. These are slotted into the frame during the manufacture of the door and quite often they shrink. They can then wobble inside the rebates and a draught can come in around the edge of the panel. Sometimes wooden panels shrink or crack along the grain or along a join where the panels were stuck together, again during manufacture. It's no good having a crack in a door or around a panel and these need to be sealed off. Paint will do it retrospectively. A sealant can be used, ideally with caulk of a similar colour to the door. We carry brown Painter's Mate sealant with us just in case we come across a problem like this, but as there are all sorts of different colours and styles of door, clear silicone often proves to be the best choice. We don't like trying to seal up cracks where wood has split, so we usually apply Sellotape over the crack and ask the customer to sort out the problem themselves by getting someone in to re-glue or repair the panel.

Insulating Windows

Double glazing is a means of insulating a window, although I much prefer triple glazing, also referred to as 3g. There are lots of different ways of doing double glazing. The most common by far is to replace the windows with new double-glazed ones. My recommendation, if you're going to do that, is to replace them with triple-glazed windows. In the past, people have sometimes kept their existing windows and added secondary double glazing. The advantage of doing this is that it's much better for noise reduction, so is frequently used near busy main roads and motorways to mitigate traffic noise. The ideal gap between windows for sound insulation is above 100mm, so you lose most or all of your window board space if you have secondary double glazing. I can foresee secondary glazing becoming much more popular in the coming years and being installed inside existing double-glazed windows to effectively upgrade them to 3g, with the added benefit of enhanced noise reduction for the building occupants.

We don't usually think of 'enhanced noise reduction' as insulation, but it is sound insulation and can be very important for some people. I myself have triple-glazed windows. They have four levels of draught seals on the windows, and they are very draughtproof. They are also great at cutting out noise, especially traffic noise from outside the house. The weight of the glass helps enormously with reducing the noise; at the same time, not having any contact between inside and outside air via draughts also cuts out a lot of noise from outside. We DraughtBusters love it when we leave a home quieter than when we arrived. So if you are hearing too much noise from outside, the first thing to do is to draughtproof, because noise is carried in through the gaps and cracks.

One of our tests during draughtproofing is the listening test. If you can hear a lot of noise from outside when all the windows are shut, the chances are that there is a direct air path from inside the room to outside. This can be where a draught seal is not actually touching the frame, where there's a gap around the frame, a trickle ventilator that won't close, a gap underneath the window board and window sill, a friction stay that is not functioning correctly and is leaving a gap on the hinge side of the window, or gaps in the window beads or rubbers. Very often with uPVC windows, the corner joints for the glazing beads are not very well made or tight; there can be a gap there which lets in a draught and noise, or the rubber gasket may have shrunk back at the corners a little bit and left a gap; again, a draught can come in there. We carry black silicone and use it to fill in those kinds of gaps, not really for soundproofing but because we hate the draughts that come in, so we do everything we possibly can to seal them out.

If you have single-glazed windows, you can do some secondary glazing with cellophane or polythene film. It's also possible to install secondary glazing using glass or Perspex sheets fixed over the frame in the winter to help keep you warmer.

There are more things that you can do to insulate windows, but these would mean that you can no longer see out of them. Shutters are a really good idea. In days gone by, some people had external shutters that they could fold across the windows from outside; these are still very common on the continent. They are mainly used to keep the heat out rather than in, and they often have louvres so that some light still comes in even when they are closed. We have seen insulated shutters on the outside of houses that fold across the outside of the window at night and insulate the window.

Again, as a leftover from bygone days, internal shutters can often be seen in stately homes, and some in more ordinary homes too, where they are designed to close across the windows on the inside at night. These usually weren't intended as insulation, but they still function as such. There's nothing to stop you standing a sheet of insulation up inside your window behind the curtains during the winter to help you stay warmer. Most sheet insulation is very light and easy to move, but a little bit bulky to store. If you do this, it will help reduce your heat loss.

We have been approached by people touting insulated linings for curtains as being the answer to the problem of heat loss in rooms. Yes, they do help, but not very much, and some of the other things mentioned above will be much more effective at reducing heat loss. Bear in mind that simply closing the curtains can reduce the heat loss in the room by 5 per cent.

Chapter Eleven

Pipework and Hot-Water Cylinders

Hot-Water Cylinders

Most hot-water cylinders now come with factory-applied spray foam insulation. In my view, this insulation is too thin. For my own home, I had a quadruple layer of spray foam applied to my new hot-water cylinder during the manufacturing process.

My recommendation for you is to add more insulation to your hot-water cylinder. This can be done by wrapping it round with old sleeping bags,

Fig 11.1 This is what a hot cylinder should not look like.

continental quilts, eiderdowns, old blankets and so on. You can even buy hot-water cylinder jackets, and I would suggest using two or three of these in addition to the spray foam insulation that it already has. If you have an older cylinder that is uninsulated, then you should certainly insulate it with at least three of these cylinder jackets. Four jackets would be even better; that would probably only give you three layers of insulation, as the diameter and height to be wrapped increases each time you add a new layer.

The hot water cylinder in Fig 11.2 is four times spray foam insulated. You might be interested to note that all the pipes that go in and out of the cylinder do so neatly on the right-hand side. They are all in a straight line, including the thermostat probes. It is a complete mystery to me why 'off-the-shelf' hot-water cylinders have pipes on diametrically opposed sides, particularly as some of the connections will be near impossible to access if they leak.

Fig 11.3 Typically, there are draughty holes around pipes and/or wires, holes with no pipes in them, and cracks. All of these need sealing.

Cold-Water Cisterns

Whether you have a cold-water store in your loft or within the house itself, it must be insulated. Insulation jackets are available for nearly all the standard sizes of cold storage cisterns; these are generally pads of fibreglass insulation encapsulated in black polythene bags that can be tied around the sides of the tank, with another one placed on top of the lid. Check the make and size of your tank before buying, as there's a variety of different shapes and sizes of cold water stores. It is crucially important that all the pipes in your loft are lagged. Preformed foam rubber pipe insulation is widely available and should be neatly fitted to all the pipes. There are various wall thicknesses available, and we suggest

Fig 11.2 An insulated hot-water cylinder.

using the thicker-walled varieties with a minimum wall thickness of 25mm.

Insulation is generally not put under water storage cisterns in lofts, and it used to be good practice not to insulate between the ceiling and the underside of the storage cistern, as this allows the little heat that escapes from the house to help take the chill off the water in the store. In my house I raised my cold-store cisterns about a metre above the loft floor to increase the pressure and consequently the flow that they were able to deliver via my gravity-fed hot- and cold-water system. I have two cold stores, one for normal water and the other for recycled rainwater. As they sit next to each other they will both be at the same temperature and so I have a thermocouple probe underneath one of them so I can see what temperature it falls to in very cold weather. Even when the outside temperature fell well below freezing, the temperature of the water in the cistern stayed well above freezing. I did not insulate underneath my cold stores but I have 500mm of loft insulation so they wouldn't gain any heat being lost from my house anyway.

Hot Pipes

Insulating hot-water or heating pipes will slow the heat loss from them but not eliminate it altogether; in fact, all the heat from hot-water piping in an insulated pipe will leak out, most likely before the next time the water is used. This renders the insulation pointless. There is an argument for insulating them in the summer, especially if the house gets too warm, because any additional source of heat in the home will tend to increase the indoor temperature even more. But even in winter, all the heat is going to leak out of the pipe through the insulation and into the house, where it will contribute to heating the home. Therefore, I do not recommend insulating hot-water pipes inside the home. Heating pipes are not used in the summer, so there is no point insulating those.

The principle here is that any heat that is lost within the heated envelope reduces the need to supply that heat from the heating system. Thus, no heat is actually being lost. Pipes in unheated areas should of course always be insulated.

The main flow-and-return pipework from the boiler to the control valves or pumps can be insulated to reasonable effect.

Outside Taps

I isolate my outside taps from inside the house during the coldest part of the winter and open them so any water in them will drip away. Plastic pipes and fittings are available for outdoor use, but these will be susceptible to damage by UV light.

Chapter Twelve

Dot-and-Dabbed Plasterboard Problems

'Dot and dab' is a technique that was developed to replace traditional wet plastering; it is now frequently used in new buildings. It became prevalent in England during the late 1970s and quickly gained in popularity due to its lower costs, faster installation, quicker drying times and ease of finishing. Walls finished in this way can be painted almost immediately. Dry lining, as the process is known, is widely used by builders and developers and is very versatile because it can be used on wood, metal stud and masonry internal partitions and ceilings, as well as on the inside of the outside walls. The ability for plasterboard to be directly adhered to masonry using dots and dabs of adhesive gives a considerable speed advantage over the wet plastering, a traditional trade that requires a high level of skill, takes longer and needs more drying out time; all of these factors make conventional plastering more expensive and far less common nowadays.

Despite its benefits, dot and dab is not without problems, however, and we will have to live with the consequences of these for generations to come.

The Downsides of Dot and Dab

Let us look at some of the downsides to the speed and apparent efficiency of dot and dab. Blockwork walls are generally built by bricklayers 'on a price', and as a result they are of a less than perfect construction, with frequent gaps and cracks that remain unfilled. These are then covered over by the plasterboard linings. When dot and dab was first introduced, cavity walls were well established but cavity fill was almost unheard of for new builds. All these cracks and gaps allow outdoor air to whistle around behind the linings, cooling them and the home they are part of. In the worst cases, there is so much thermal bypass, as it is known, that the householders are effectively living in plasterboard tents. Energy was cheap and plentiful and insulation levels were poor in the days when these houses were built.

More recently, best practice has dictated additional measures that should be used when dry lining. A requirement to use full ribbons of adhesive around the perimeter of each wall was introduced to try to prevent the problem of air leaking in behind the linings. This was a bodged solution to a known serious problem that should have been properly addressed at that point in time. The tradesmen, again, were generally working to a fixed price, and as this method takes longer and uses more materials, it was rarely done in this way: it is almost impossible to find any of these ribbons today. They would show up on thermal imaging, but I have never yet seen any on my or other people's thermal images. Checking that the regulations have been adhered to is very difficult and so it tends not to happen.

At some point somebody realised that this was a problem and decided to ask for the blockwork to be sealed with a parge coat, a thin coating of a flexible plaster that seals all the gaps and cracks in the blockwork, before the linings are applied. This is rarely seen in practice either. Sales of parge coat have risen but not nearly enough to impact on future problems. Furthermore, there is typically a gap left at the bottom of the wall, between the plasterboard and the floor, that allows draughts to enter the rooms.

Recently, airtightness testing of new homes has been introduced, but unfortunately a room or even a whole house can be reasonably airtight yet still have all the problems highlighted above. The recommendation that the skirting boards should be sealed to the floor is questionable, even though it is one of the so called 'robust details'. Other recommendations include sealing all internal visible cracks and gaps to give an airtight layer inside the home. Each room in the home becomes more airtight, but air is still able to waft around behind the linings and inside the insulation barrier.

I wrote an article on this subject for *Green Building* magazine in summer 2013 after a diligent homeowner discovered that warm air was emanating from gaps behind his plasterboard linings and leaking into his loft. The story got worse when it was discovered that cold air could travel from under the suspended concrete ground floor, up the back of the ground-floor wall linings, and into the first-floor void. From there it could continue up behind the first-floor wall linings, being joined on its way by cold air coming in from outside through the many cracks and gaps in the blockwork and around the joist ends in the void. Most people do not notice this air movement, which, even on still days, is driven by convection currents, although you may have noticed draughts emanating from electrical socket outlets.

Having discovered that air was circulating behind the linings, a spot temperature survey of the main bedroom was performed. This revealed that there was an 11° temperature gradient between the bottom of the walls and the top. The bedroom was partly above a garage, but the floor had been well insulated. The bottoms of the walls were thought to be below dew point, at least some of the time. However, there were some areas, mainly in the corners of window reveals, where mould was evident.

The reason there was no condensation at skirting level was most likely because it was so draughty down there that even if droplets did form, they would evaporate away again almost immediately, as the drier outside air passed over them, stirring and mixing with the warmer air in the room. Not only were the draughts moving behind the linings, but they were coming out under skirtings, even on internal walls, through downlighter holes in the ground floor ceilings, around pipes, out of switches and even from behind architraves. The owner described his

Fig 12.1 This is the gap between the edge of the plasterboard ceiling and the blockwork wall. It is possible to see the top of the wall lining board and the gap behind it, which was allowing warm air to flow continuously up into the loft, resulting in high heat losses.

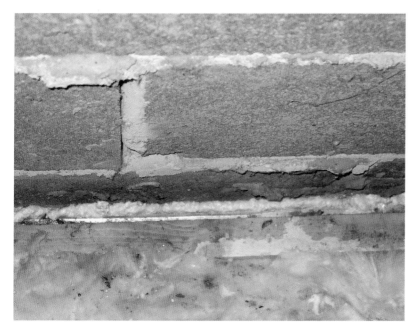

Fig 12.2 The gap now filled with foam. All the other homes in the same development will need to have this process carried out, but the residents are unaware of the problem. The gap varied from 12mm up to about 20mm depending on how straight the walls and blockwork were.

house as 'a colander' on several occasions. He went on to do a truly magnificent job of sealing up all the draughts at floor and ceiling levels both upstairs and downstairs.

Fig 12.3 below is a thermal image of a wall that has been dry lined using the notorious dot and dab method. The blue-coloured patches indicate that they are cold and dark blue very cold. There is a plethora of problems that the image highlights so it makes a good quiz – how many problems can you identify in this thermal image?

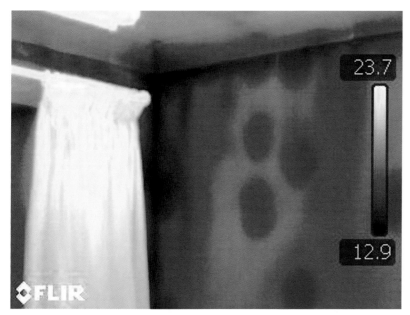

Fig 12.3 Thermal image of a dot-and-dabbed lounge wall. Note that the dots are showing up as colder than the wall due to conduction through the adhesive. It is clear that ribbons of adhesive were not used; we can see cold air is infiltrating at the top of the walls and blowing over the edges of the ceiling. There are lots of problems at the corner of the room.

Skirtings

Skirtings, especially in dry-lined homes, can frequently be draughty. As the blockwork is rarely sealed, draughts can come in through the blockwork itself, through gaps and cracks and holes that have been left anywhere behind the dry lining, and although they can't get out through the linings themselves, they can get out around the edges. Their best chance of getting out into the house is by going under the skirting board. Our suggestion is that, if you have a dry-lined house, the number one action is to remove the skirtings and fill the gaps with foam all the way along between the floor and the dry linings as in Fig 12.5. Then, when the foam has set, cut it off flush with the wall as in Fig 12.6, and then fill any holes that remain with decorator's caulk or a similar filler and refit the skirtings.

There is a set of 'robust details' recommended as a cure for air leakage in modern homes that specifies the skirting boards should be sealed to the floor! I have a problem with this because although the

Fig 12.4 This hole was behind a skirting board. It is directly joined to the underfloor void, and this is the same as to the outside world! There is more information on how to resolve problems like this in Chapter 9.

Fig 12.5 Foam filling the gap between the floor and the back of the dry linings.

room becomes somewhat more airtight by sealing the skirting to the floor, it doesn't prevent the cold air from blowing around behind the dry linings. Our suggestion of filling the gap between the dry lining and the floor instead stops air from being able to come up through the floor and get behind the dry linings and out from behind the skirting at the same time.

The next place to look for air infiltration is between the ceiling and first floor; *see* Chapter 13.

Fig 12.6 Excess foam cut off flush, ready for skirting to be refitted.

Chapter Thirteen

The First-Floor Void

In the void between the ground-floor ceiling and the first-floor floorboards there is often a plethora of problems. Draughts or wind from outside can blow in through small gaps between blocks or bricks, and through cracks to the sides of and above floor joists. The latter result from the fact that the joists can shrink by up to 8mm in height and by up to 3mm in width. The blockwork is not always fully filled with mortar; there is often none between the 'good' end of a block and a joist, some may be missing from perpendicular joints (the vertical mortar joints) and there are often gaps around service penetrations. It is easier to see this in the pictures.

ABOVE LEFT: Fig 13.1 A gap between the blocks in the floor void that should fill the space between the joists. Note that the bricks of the outside skin and the mortar bed joint between them should not be visible; the cavity batts were not installed properly, thus adding to the problems. This is the kind of gap that a mouse could use to gain access to the floor void; from there it would be able to get to other places in the house too.

ABOVE RIGHT: Fig 13.2 A shrinkage gap beside a joist. As the joist shrinks during the initial drying-out process, the gap opens up and is now clearly letting a draught in.

Fig 13.3 Gaps to the side of and above a floor joist.

Fig 13.4 Gap above a floor joist allowing draughts into the floor void and under the skirting, and also, in this case, up behind the plasterboard linings.

Fig 13.5 This is why most cavity-walled homes in the UK are so cold and draughty. Outdoor air gains access to the void between the ceiling and the first-floor floorboards. This happens all the way round the house, causing massive heat losses. The draughts have access to the heart of the house and the result is cold, draughty homes that use far more energy than they would if these draughts weren't there.

Fig 13.6 Newly sealed-in joist end. This is only the first stage of our suggested airtightness improvement works.

Rectifying the Problems

The sequence of pictures here is a case study on how to rectify the problems in your first-floor void. They will be of particular interest to people who live in dry-lined homes, but all first-floor voids have similar problems and all need to be treated as detailed here. The first stage is to gain access to the floor void beside an outside wall.

The upshot of all this is that if you live in a cavity-walled house and haven't yet sealed the perimeter of your first-floor void, then you might as well be living in a bungalow with no loft insulation, sitting under a second bungalow, containing the bedrooms and bathroom, with an uninsulated and draughty floor. This was a quote that I first heard at a meeting at the Building Research Establishment in the late 1980s; it is such a shame that these problems are continuing unchecked.

Fig 13.7 Here is an open gap between the edge of the ground-floor ceiling and the blockwork. These gaps can vary in size from a few millimetres to large enough to accommodate pipes; see, for example, Fig 13.12.

Fig 13.8 Seal the gap between the ground-floor wall lining board and the blockwork by filling the gap between the edge of the ceiling and the blocks with foam.

Fig 13.9 Add a board to seal any gaps or cracks in or around the blocks. Any sheet material will do.

Fig 13.10 A piece of plasterboard 'buttered up' ready to be pressed into place.

Fig 13.11 The final step is to seal around the sheet and then up behind the plasterboard above (that is yet to be done in this picture).

Fig 13.12 Here the void between the wall and the lining is wide enough to allow uninsulated pipes to fit into it. Plenty of draughts were blowing up the gap as it was connected to the void below the ground floor.

Fig 13.13 Pipes foamed around prior to sealing the blockwork.

Fig 13.14 Retrofitted wiring with the back of the coving visible. Note that the gap between the top of the wall lining and the blockwork has been foam sealed across the top in this dry-lined home. We would also seal the air path between the floor void and the void that leads into the space behind the coving to prevent air infiltration.

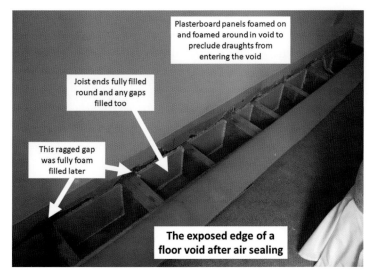

Plasterboard panels foamed on and foamed around in void to preclude draughts from entering the void

Joist ends fully filled round and any gaps filled too

This ragged gap was fully foam filled later

The exposed edge of a floor void after air sealing

Fig 13.15 The next job is to foam from the top of the new boards up to behind the bottom of the bedroom wall lining sheets. Once this is done, the floorboards can be refixed and skirtings refitted. Finally, the carpet can be put back in place.

Fig 13.16 This is a 1980s house near Eastbourne. How much energy has this wedge cost? And how many people saw it and ignored it during construction? The floor joist may well have twisted while lying in the sun and so needed to be wedged back to straighten it up before fixing the flooring, which is good practice but why didn't anyone fill the gap?

Fig 13.17 Another example, from Jeff of Green Building Forum fame, diligently sealing between his joist ends with sheet insulation and foam.

Preventative Measures

Joist Boots

Joist ends can be set into plastic joist boots. The idea of these is that they prevent air infiltration around the end of the joists. While they do achieve that, they don't prevent air infiltration through the blockwork or through the gap between the joist boot and the blockwork, however, although they do make it a little bit more difficult for air to sneak in that way.

The main downside of joist boots is that they have a flange all around them. This interferes with plastering the wall and often causes patches to drop off under every joist, as the boot moves slightly when someone walks on the floor upstairs, or when the plaster does not adhere very well to the plastic. In practice, they are so little used that it is difficult to find them built into a house.

The Tony Tray

Traditionally, when we have built houses, we have built in massive air-leakage paths in the void between the ground floor ceiling and the first floor floorboards. The solution described here is only applicable for new builds and was first published in *Green Building* magazine in summer 2013.

Building in floor joists gives rise to a plethora of problems. Draughts enter this void around the joist ends and through the infill blockwork and mortar joints. Later, as the timbers shrink due to drying out, more leakage paths open and existing ones become larger. The draughts (sometimes gales) resulting from these air-leakage paths are massive and are getting right into our homes from an area where it is very difficult to carry out remedial work due to inaccessibility.

We say that we would like to build tight. I would like to see us get it right first time. We need in some way to draughtproof this area when it is built, allowing for shrinkage of joists (joist hangers do not solve the problem and add unnecessary cost and potential problems from squeaks and creaks). The solution should be simple and easy to do. It should be built in as we go, cheap and essentially failsafe.

It's no use talking without suggesting a remedy. So here it is:

1. Set the joists on a breathable windproof membrane.

Fig 13.18 The solution for joists. This applies to all joists – wooden, composite, beams for beam and block, and concrete planks.

2. Build in the joists with blockwork infill.
3. Flap the membrane up over the joist ends, protecting a 75mm flap on top of the floor or joists with a length of 25 × 75mm timber.
4. Repeat the process all around the house, parallel with, as well as perpendicular to, the joists.
5. Provide any service ducts through the barrier in readiness for future use and seal them to the membrane.
6. Seal the joins in the membrane (by welting or taping; corners are best folded with no cuts or joins) and ensure all the joins and corners are air leakage tight.

7. Later in the building process, fix expanded metal over the flaps of the membrane, up the wall behind the skirting and at the top of the walls just below the ceiling.

On wet plastering, an airtight seal will be formed (in my opinion, the dot and dabbing on of plasterboard is not an acceptable option in a well-built house).

The plugging-up of this area is something we should have done long ago. My hope is that the above will enable us to head towards building for a future where airtightness is the norm.

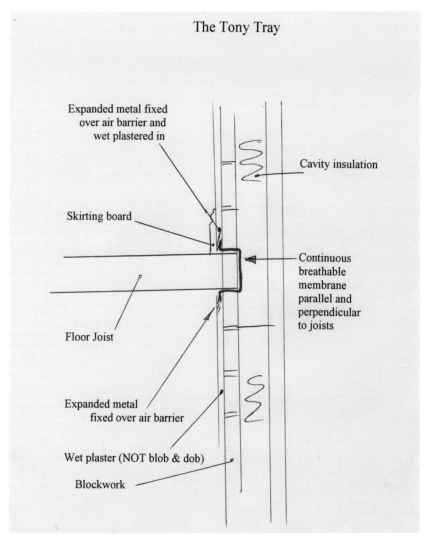

The Tony Tray

Expanded metal fixed over air barrier and wet plastered in

Cavity insulation

Skirting board

Continuous breathable membrane parallel and perpendicular to joists

Floor Joist

Expanded metal fixed over air barrier

Wet plaster (NOT blob & dob)

Blockwork

Fig 13.19 Section through the Tony Tray.

Chapter Fourteen

Draughtproofing Sliding Sash Windows

Sliding sash windows were the windows of choice during the Victorian era, and many terraced houses still have their original ones in use today. In fact, some estate agents treat them as something rather special and desirable when houses come onto the market. There are many very good things about sliding sash windows but there are also some downsides.

Benefits of Sash Windows

Among the major factors in their favour, they tend to be set back into the brickwork of the house and are therefore protected slightly more from the elements than a window which is built into the outside skin of a house, as is almost universal nowadays. They were constructed using much higher-quality timber than is available today; it also stayed drier because some areas of sliding sash windows don't get painted, which allows the wood nearby to dry out if by chance it does get damp.

For instance, parts of the side rails of the sashes are never painted as they are inside a channel formed by the parting beads and can only be painted if you take the window out; then when you put it back in again, it would jam badly on the paint. The sides of the frame behind the parting beads and the channels in which the sash runs are part of a box section, within which the weights that counterbalance the windows slide up and down. There is nothing else inside that box and it is also never painted; it is also well ventilated, so the wood that faces into the box is always dry and never rots.

The top rail of the top sash never gets wet, but even if it did, it could dry out upwards because the top is also never painted. The top rail of the bottom sash is inside the bottom rail of the top sash, and that rail never gets wet apart from when somebody washes the windows, so that rail also will never decay. The bottom rail of the bottom sash should, if properly constructed, have a chamfer on the bottom edge so that water can drip away from the front edge; the underside should not be painted and that helps the bottom rail of the bottom sash to remain dry. Unless somebody has painted the underneath of the bottom rail then it remains rot-free.

The sill of a sliding sash box frame is usually made from higher-quality wood than the rest of the window; sometimes it is oak but if not, it might be pitch pine or yellow pine; although this member can rot, even now, few of them have yet succumbed. Another reason that the window frames don't decay is that they are built into masonry, typically brickwork, which has been built using lime mortar. This is very good at stopping wood from rotting, as it draws any moisture out of the wood and into the mortar and then ventilates it away, keeping the wood dry and free from rot.

Draughts – the Disadvantage of Sash Windows

The main downside of sliding sash windows is that they are often draughty, if not very draughty. They don't have draught seals and usually they don't fit terribly well, especially if they're over a hundred years old. The box mentioned above, in which the weights slide up and down, is open to the elements via the pulleys, and wind can whistle out from these, especially the one for the bottom sash. Considerable draughts can emanate from that pulley.

The sashes themselves are draughty all round – top, bottom and middle – as wood simply meets wood. The mid-rail should have a cam-shaped latch that squeezes the top and bottom sash together. This does a very good job of stopping a draught from the mid-rail but generally I find that it is either non-functional or the window is clogged up with paint, so there's always a gap across that mid-rail allowing a draught to come in. The top and the bottom can both be draughty because they don't have any draught strips and, with wood-on-wood contact, they are sometimes not quite square and may rattle a little bit in the wind. The sides of both sashes, as mentioned before, run up and down in an unpainted groove. There is a gap between the sashes and the beads, and draughts can enter through these gaps.

Fig 14.1 Side of a sliding sash window looking at the sash box, pulley, and top sash.

Unfortunately, this is not the only place where draughts can come in. Often the pointing between the frame and the masonry or brickwork has, to some extent, parted company with the window frame or even fallen out altogether, allowing a draught in behind the box frame. Once it's in there, it can get inside the box and then come out behind the architrave, into the room above the top architrave, and more rarely underneath the little sill on the inside of the window. We have even seen draughts between the glass and the wooden frame, where the putty or bedding has cracked and fallen out. I have always painted my window sills and the bottom rails of all sashes and fanlights twice as often as the rest of my windows. We have seen cracked glass, sometimes letting in draughts through gaps a few millimetres wide. Sliding sash windows are very draughty.

Remedial Measures

All is not lost, however. Sliding sash windows can be draughtproofed retrospectively. There are many companies that will come out and apply draught strips. They insert brush strips into the top rail of the top sash, the bottom rail of the bottom sash and the mid-rail where the two sashes meet. To do this, they have to take the sashes out; they will normally replace the sash cords when they put them back in again, which is a very good thing to have done. Then either the parting beads or the staff beads are replaced with new ones with integral brush strips. Whichever method is used, it means that the sides of both sashes are nicely draught sealed. One thing they don't usually do is to draughtproof the pulleys. We often just push a piece of tissue paper into this hole as a temporary measure because the windows aren't opened very often during the winter; the tissue paper just falls out when somebody moves the window in the spring and another piece can be pushed in for the following winter.

There is a lot of good information about sliding sash windows on the Historic England website (historiceng-land.org.uk). You can also find videos of how to do the works on YouTube, and we have a little bit of information about this on the DraughtBusters website as well.

Another downside of sliding sash windows is that they are only single glazed. This is not too much of a problem because draughtproofing is far more important than double or even triple glazing. Sliding sash windows can be upgraded to double glazed relatively easily, even within conservation areas, by using so-called Slimlite double-glazed units, which are composed of two sheets of 3mm glass and a narrow 4mm spacer bar. If you go down this route, you will have to either change from sash weights to spiral balances or upgrade the sash weights by making them heavier so that they can counterbalance the additional weight of glass. This is worth doing, but only if you're going to draughtproof the window too.

It is possible to replace sliding sash windows with new windows that look almost identical from outside; even uPVC ones can have the divided glazing bars and little features on the top sash that are almost iconic for sliding sash windows. The lifetime of a plastic window is very short in comparison to the life of a building, and it would seem rather a shame to replace a 100-year-old window with a plastic one that's not going to last as well, but the choice is yours. In the past we have replaced sliding sash windows with new wooden versions that have come pre-glazed, decorated and fully ready to install. They have very good ironmongery and may have tilt mechanisms so that they can be cleaned from indoors, and may be double or triple glazed.

In short, a good plan of action if you have sash windows would have three steps:

1. Draughtproof.
2. Seal all around frame.
3. Install secondary glazing.

Draughtproofing

It is not as easy as you might think to draughtproof a sliding sash window. We have offered some advice, but this may well prove either too expensive or too difficult to do, so here are some simple and cheaper methods. Each window usually has two sliding sashes, and in a lot of cases, one of these can be sealed shut. We recommend using decorator's caulk or acrylic sealant, both of which can be removed using hot water, so this process is reversible. We recommend sealing from the inside; if there are small children around, then seal the bottom sash to the frame on both sides and across the bottom. Alternatively, the top sash can be sealed in a similar way.

If there are small children in the house and you're concerned about them getting out of windows, it's also possible to fit a stop that only allows the bottom sash to open 100mm. Simple rubber door stops screwed into the channel at the right place will perform this function perfectly adequately. We then recommend sealing up the holes above and below the pulley, where draughts can enter, with something that is easy to remove, such as a piece of screwed-up polythene or tissue pushed in.

Only one sash can now have draughts, but they can come in all the way around it. You may wish to use some form of draught strip, but an alternative is simply to push tissue paper in all around the sash, including across the middle rail, when it's very cold or very windy. This will probably fall out if you do open the window, and certainly you can take it out in spring and autumn, but it will be very helpful during the very cold parts of the winter. You should open a window in a room for a few minutes every day, but you may be able to get away without opening the window if you open all the doors, plus a window upstairs, and try to blow air through; this is known as purge ventilation. There is more advice on ventilation in Chapter 3.

Sealing all around Frame

Even if you have undertaken all the measures above, you will find draughts come in through all sorts of other places. Next, we are going to consider draughts that come in over, under and around the frame. You need to check and make sure that the architraves up and down each side are attached to the wall. There may well be a crack between the architrave and the wall or between the architrave and some filler that others have applied in the past, which now has a gap. We recommend that such a crack is filled with decorator's caulk or acrylic sealant. You should also check across the top of the frame above the architrave and see that there are no cracks there. There may well be, but they will be smaller.

Let us consider for a moment how sash windows were fitted. When Victorian terraced houses were built, construction was much more like a factory production line. Specialists would come in and do their part and materials were often brought in down temporary railway tracks laid down the middle of the road so that a steam-driven crane could be used to ferry materials down the road – ballast, cement, bricks, timber, slates, windows and so on. They laid the drains and foundations first, then the brickwork and roof.

The windows were fitted later into preformed openings which were smaller on the outside than on the inside. There would be a wooden lintel above the window opening, typically a piece of 'four by three' softwood, and the outside skin would carry the load, using either a brick arch or some form of stone lintel. The sash box windows would be carried into the building in one piece with the sashes and weights already in them, but probably not glazed at this stage. The inside faces of the sash boxes had pieces of wood that projected up above the top of the window, usually about 100mm, and the window would be offered up into the opening and wedged into position, so that the sill was sitting exactly on top of the stone or concrete sill that was built into the outside skin. This usually had a water bar already in it, which would sit about 25mm back behind the outside skin brickwork; there would be a drip slot cut into the bottom sill that would be located over this water bar. This stopped water running under the window and off the back of the sill.

The builders would double-check that the window was completely square and upright; they would then fix through the pieces of wood that run up onto the lintel with just one or two cut nails each side. That is all that fixed the frame in place! (I know this because I've taken lots of sash windows out, and the way that we would do it is to lever the bottom of the window towards the room. We would then lift it upwards and into the room. This would disconnect the cut nails that were used to hold the top to the lintel.) The window would then be parged internally and pointed outside. Plastering would take place on the inside, and finally, architraves would be fitted to master the gaps.

Often, we would find that the window had moved very slightly and that the pointing on the outside had been replaced several times. Gaps behind the architraves would open up and plaster under the sill might detach. The top usually didn't have any problems, but you can often see the two bits of projecting wood through the plaster because they only have a thin skim of plaster over them.

It's important to realise that draughts can come in right round the outside of the sash boxes and then behind the architrave and into the room. It's also important that you seal all these gaps up. We recommend fixing the bottoms of sash window boxes to the reveals with screws and brackets to stop them creeping inwards and allowing new draughts to enter the room.

Secondary Glazing

There is one more thing that you can do to help reduce your energy use, once you have carried out all the steps above, and that is to secondary glaze your sliding sash windows. If you completely cover both sashes with secondary glazing, this should stop all the draughts coming into the room. The cheapest way to do this is to use a shrink film stretched over the staff beads and tightened up using warm air from a hairdryer. You can buy kits to do this. It is a temporary solution, but it does work well.

The next option would be to buy some clear Perspex or polycarbonate sheet measured to go 20mm beyond the parting beads all round. Stick on some foam draught-sealing strips next to the parting beads, then clip down the edges of the glazing sheet with small screws in cable clips or other suitable clips. Alternatively, you can use self-adhesive magnetic strips right around the outside line of the staff beads, and another strip right around the outside edge of your glazing sheet to hold it in position. You can remove it during the warmer months and stand it behind a cupboard or the sofa ready for next year.

The next step up is to use a sheet of toughened glass. This can be quite big and a little bit cumbersome but the best way to use it is to go right round the edge of it with a piece of clear plastic tube, cut so that it fits over the edge of the glass, and then clip it to the frame using cable clips as above, with small screws in them. You can buy kits that will help you do this, but you'll have to buy the glass separately. We strongly recommend using toughened glass, probably 4mm thick. Again, you can store it behind a cupboard or the sofa after the cold weather has passed so that you can open the windows in the summer.

Further Considerations

Some sliding sash windows have shutters built in next to them. These are often hinged and fold away very neatly. They may not necessarily be recognised as shutters as they may be painted so that they don't move at all. Shutters are very nice as they reduce heat loss and draughts, but they have drawbacks too. The shutter boxes are connected to the sash boxes that are at the sides of the window, and the sash boxes are draughty. There's plenty of room for draughts to get through the cracks and in at the corners where they've been nailed; there can also be knotholes, splits and other damage that allows draughts to come in. The problem now is that the shutters are probably fitted into recessed boxes and connected directly to all these potential draughts. What happens is that the

draughts come out into the recess where the internal shutters are stored. They can get behind that recess and come out between the framing and the architrave or between the framing and the wall. You will need to seal all around inside the recess to make sure no draughts can come out between the box architrave and the wall.

The sash window may also have some form of panelling beneath it. This looks nice, but it will have been fixed when the window was fitted, probably before plastering, and is almost certainly going to have draughts running around behind it and trying to get out all around it. So, under your window, between you and the outside world, is a very thin piece of wood with no insulation and no draughtproofing. Draughts and wind can blow from under the floor if it's a ground floor, up the back of this panel, and then get out into the room. Further draughts can come in under the window or through the sash boxes and in behind this panel, and again get out into the room.

If you have such panels, it will be a labour of love to try to seal up all the air paths from outside the house to behind these panels, as well as the ones that go from there into your room. One of my friends removed his panels and shutter recesses and insulated behind them. He foam sealed all the gaps, refitted them all and then redecorated. He couldn't fit very much insulation in, but something is better than nothing.

Looking after Wooden Windows

It's always worth looking after wooden windows very carefully. To this end, the first thing to do is to make sure that the paint film is intact and not peeling or flaking. Ensure that the corner joints of the sashes are close fitting. It is extremely common to find that these joints are open, and even a gap of half a millimetre will allow water to get into the joint every time it rains; this will cause the wood to get wet and it will soon start to rot. You do not need to take the window sash out to resolve this problem: with modern wood glues, it is very easy to introduce some glue into the crack and then use a small ratchet strap to pull the joint back together again. If you do this when you first notice the gap, it will go back very easily; if it's been there a while, try ratchet strapping it before you apply the glue, then let the pressure off and introduce the glue. Our favourite type of glue is foaming wood glue, available under various brand names. Other glues will also work, including PVA, though a waterproof version of PVA may be a better choice.

If the wood on your windows appears to have deformed underneath the paint this is quite bad news, and indicates your windows haven't been looked after quite well enough. When wood rots it changes shape; once this happens, it becomes quite expensive to repair the window as it needs to be taken away to a joinery shop and a new rail – or possibly more than just a rail – added.

A lot of older wooden windows, including sliding sash windows, have putty that helps to seal the glass to the frame. With age, putties can shrink and crack and pull away from both the frame and the glass. When this happens, water can sit on the bottom rail of the sash, which is the last thing that we want, so putties should be kept in good condition; to look after them we usually paint over them and very slightly onto the glass.

The next point is a very important one, but is overlooked by all but the most conscientious of sliding sash window owners. When the window was glazed, a bed of putty was applied all around the rebate; the glass would have been firmly pressed into this, and a little bit of it would have squeezed out inside. The glazier's next task would have been to put glazing sprigs into the frame to hold the glass firmly in place, usually one or two to each edge of the glass. Then the putty would have been applied to the outside, using a beautifully clean putty knife to squeeze it in and give it a lovely smooth finish. The glazier would have neatly cut off the surplus inside and kept it for reuse.

I have talked about the putty decaying on the outside of the window, but most people don't realise that the putty on the inside of the window needs to be maintained too, especially across the bottom of the glass. The reason for this is that almost certainly at some times of the year, you will get condensation on the inside of your windows, and it will run down and sit on top of the bottom rail; if the putty is gone, it will soak into the bottom rail. It will then get damp and start to decay. We don't object to a bead of silicone across the bottom of the inside of the glass on a sliding sash window; there are silicones available that can be painted over as well, and these would be recommended for this application.

We have mentioned already that often the underside of the bottom sash rail is not painted, so that if it does get at all damp, the wood has a chance to dry out. Indeed, not painting undersides behind the drip

Fig 14.2 Window showing distress on the sill and ledge. These should be fully prepared and painted, bare wood primed, filled, sanded, undercoated, and given two full coats of gloss. This applies to the bottom rails too. Note that the window sashes are both painted shut. Any gaps should be filled and painted over. There are opening casements above for ventilation.

line is a very good way of keeping joinery dry, and hence preserving it. Other places where this can be done are beneath projecting windowsills, the bottoms of doors and weather bars and all casement windows behind the drip line.

Sash cords should be replaced regularly. If you do this, they won't break, and you can control when you have to change them. If you wait until they break, they can be repaired by carefully removing the parting bead in order to access the pocket at the bottom of the inside of the frame; this usually just fits in using wood joints and gravity to hold it there and it is not nailed or glued in. This will give you access to the sash weights. You might as well replace both cords every time you open a pocket. You can find a useful video about how to replace sash cords on YouTube (https://youtu.be/HB_a3nNoFs0). It really isn't difficult and used to be a homeowner's job, but now most people get a specialist in to do it for them.

ABOVE LEFT: Fig 14.3 This window needs a little bit of re-puttying, and the sash could do with repainting. The sill is already a replacement but needs the same process as the window in Fig 14.2. We would check under the sill to make sure that it is sealed to the stone sill 40mm or 50mm back.

FAR LEFT: Fig 14.4 Sliding sash window with no draught strips. We can see that here the sash cords are in good condition, though they often fail at the point where they are tied onto the sash weight inside the sash box.

LEFT: Fig 14.5 Note that draughts can emanate from the holes and gaps around this pulley. We usually suggest wedging tissue paper into the holes above and below the pulley and to each side of it for the coldest part of the winter season.

Every little action counts, so even if you have only managed to take one or two small steps to reduce your draughts, those were good things to do. Draught-proofing is cost-effective and simple, so even if you can't do it yourself, you should ask a friend or relative to do it for you. When we can combine saving energy with saving money that is a double whammy, but to be warmer into the bargain makes it a triple whammy.

We have a mountain to climb, and unlike normal mountains ours is getting higher! There are more poorly constructed houses being built and the existing housing stock is getting older, little by little decaying and becoming draughtier. Our hope is that by raising the profile of draughtproofing, as we have in this book, that mountain will reduce in height and the problems will become fewer.

Air barrier A barrier that prevents outdoor air or wind from entering a building

Air brick A perforated brick used for ventilation, usually under timber floors, in rooms or in roof spaces

Airtightness The elimination of all unintended gaps and cracks in the external envelope of the building

Airtightness test The recognised method used to determine the total amount of air lost through leaks in a building's fabric

Architrave The moulded frame around a doorway or window

Beam and block floor A floor constructed of pre-stressed concrete floor beams, incorporating concrete blocks

Bird's mouth rafter A rafter with a notch cut into it to fit neatly over a wall plate, allowing the weight of the rafter to be carried vertically

Boiler flue A pipe that carries the exhaust gases produced by a boiler out of the home and releases them into the atmosphere

Brush strip A strip made of durable synthetic materials in the form of a brush used to help stop draughts

Cavity wall insulation Insulated material used to fill the cavity wall, usually polystyrene beads, foam, fibreglass or rockwool

Ceiling rose The part of a light fitting that encases the cable and supports the hanging filament

Ceiling tie The lowest member of a truss, usually horizontal, which carries the ceiling construction, storage loads and water tank

Chimney balloon An inflatable bag or wad that effectively blocks the chimney, stopping warm air from escaping and cold air from getting in

Cold roof A roof where the insulation is fitted between the rafters/structure, with the roof substrate or deck fitted above the insulation

Condensation The process that induces water vapour in the air to turn into liquid. Condensation will occur on cold surfaces in winter

Condensing boiler A boiler that extracts additional heat from the flue gases by causing them to condense within the boiler itself

Damp-proof course A barrier, usually formed by a membrane, built into the walls of a property

Damp Slightly wet, especially in a way that is not pleasant or comfortable

Dot and dab A method used to install sheets of insulation or plasterboard. Dots of adhesive are dabbed on walls or surfaces during the process onto which the sheets are stuck

Downlighter A light fitting installed into a ceiling rather than attached to it

Draught excluder Most often used to refer to something that prevents draughts coming under doors

Draught seal Often used to refer to the black rubber strips used in UPVC windows and doors to exclude draughts

Draught strip A strip of rubber or nylon brush, either self-adhesive or in a plastic or aluminium carrier, used to stop draughts getting into buildings around windows or doors

Dry lining A method used to line blockwork walls with plasterboard

Escutcheon A flat piece of metal for protection and often ornamentation, to cover a keyhole; in our case, ideally one that prevents draughts

External wall insulation A layer of insulation that's fixed to the outside of a wall

Extractor fan A fan that extracts air from the hot or humid places in your house and sends it outside

First-floor void The void between the ground-floor ceiling and the floor above it

Floor screed A thin layer of material that is placed on top of a concrete subfloor

Friction stay A modern form of a window hinge that allows a window to remain open in any open position

Gable wall A triangular section of wall at the end of a pitched roof

Galleried ceiling A ceiling that follows the pitch of a roof; may also be known as a cathedral or vaulted ceiling

Glazing gasket Used to hold glass tight against a window frame or bead, most often made of black rubber

Hipped roof Where all the roof slopes go downwards to the walls without having gables

In-house winter cooling system Anything that acts inside your home to cool it during the winter

Insulation Material used to significantly reduce heat lost or gained by buildings

Internal wall insulation Used on the inside of external walls to improve indoor comfort and reduce energy use

Noggin A strut used to give rigidity to a framework, typically fixed between joists or studs to increase their strength and stiffness

Oversite A layer of concrete that is used to create the ground floor of a house

Parge coat A thin coat of cement or mortar used to prepare or windproof masonry walls

Parting beads In a sliding sash window, a vertical strip of wood that is fitted between the upper and lower sashes. It creates a channel for the sashes to slide past each other.

Party wall A dividing partition between two adjoining buildings that is shared by both properties

Perp end joints Perpendicular end joints are the vertical joints between blocks or bricks that have been laid in a horizontal course to form a wall

Polystyrene, extruded and expanded Expanded polystyrene is generally small light balls that get everywhere unless compressed and stuck together into white or grey sheets. Extruded polystyrene is this same product but heated and foamed up to form it into blue or pink sheets

Purge ventilation Manually controlled ventilation of rooms or spaces at a relatively high rate to rapidly dilute pollutants and/or water vapour; may be provided by natural or mechanical means

Radiant barrier A type of building material that reflects thermal radiation and reduces heat transfer

Rebate A recess or groove cut into the edge of a piece of machinable material, usually wood – in the case of a glazing rebate, to accept and house the edge of a piece of glass or glazing unit

R-value A measure of the ability of insulation materials to resist heat flow

Sarking Something laid across roof rafters before the roof coverings are applied; it can be rolled out (such as roofing felt, a breather membrane) or may be lengths or sheets of wood

Sash box A box on the side of a sash window where a system of weights and pulleys on a piece of sash cord counterbalances the sash

Sealant A silicone or acrylic mastic used for sealing areas that need a waterproof or airproof seal

Secondary glazing An additional pane of glass (and frame) added to an existing window

Skeiling The raked (angled) part of a ceiling sometimes found at the perimeter of a top floor room, being the plastered underside of the principal roof rafters. These are found where the ceilings are set at a level higher than the tops of the external walls

Sliding sash window A window where the sashes slide, generally vertically over one another

Sloping soffit A section of ceiling that follows the line of the underside of roof rafters, often at the edge of a ceiling

Stud wall A frame of timber or metal studs secured to the floor, ceiling and walls, which is then generally covered with plasterboard

Thermal bridging The movement of heat across a building element that is more conductive than the materials around it

Thermal bypass When heat is transferred around the insulation

Thermal image A method of measuring the temperatures of surfaces using infrared radiation to create an electronic image

Trickle ventilator A device usually fitted at the top of a window that allows fresh air to circulate naturally through a room, and allows used air out

Truss A prefabricated structural frame that is used to support the roof of a building; it can also be a large structural frame that forms the main structure of a roof

U-value A measure of the total resistance of a building element like a wall to the passage of heat through it

Ventilation The circulation of air throughout a building

Wall plate A horizontal member, usually wood, laid along the top of a wall to support joists, rafters or trusses

Wall ties These are used to join the two leaves of a cavity wall together. Hidden from view after construction, wall ties play a vital role in ensuring the stability of a building

Warm roof Where the insulation layer is laid on top of the roof deck, so called because the roof structure and its substrate are on the warm side of the insulation

Weather bar A bar that prevents water being blown in under a door or window sill

Wind washing Wind-driven air movement through or behind thermal insulation

Window board A board that closes over the cavity between the window and the front of the internal wall

Window reveal The surround through the wall inside a window opening

Wing insulation Insulation outside the footprint of the floor of a building that increases the path length of escaping heat

Tools and Materials

Tools

Somewhat surprisingly, by far the most useful tool is a pair of scissors! These can be used for a variety of purposes, not least for opening packaging. Even a simple job like fitting draught strips becomes much easier if you use a pair of scissors to cut the strip to length into the corner or at the end of a rebate. A Stanley knife really doesn't work well for this task and it's very easy to have a mishap while using one.

The next most useful tool is a green/yellow sponge kitchen scouring pad. We get through quite a lot of these cleaning rebates before fitting draught strips. A caulking gun is needed to seal up cracks and gaps. They are not very easy to use but I have had years of practice and I find that the younger generation take to them like ducks to water. It is all about hand-eye coordination. We also carry a set of general small hand tools.

Basic Draughtproofing Toolkit

- Scissors
- Scouring sponge pad
- Cloth
- Caulking gun
- Infrared thermometer
- Knife
- Screwdrivers
- Hammer
- Torch
- Tape measure
- Junior hacksaw
- Pliers

Materials

Draught strips come in a wide variety of shapes and sizes, and unfortunately one size does not fit all gaps. We carry a range of self-adhesive strips: foam ones in tiny, small, medium, large and jumbo sizes in white and brown, both colours of nylon brush strips and butyl rubber 'P' and 'E' strips. We sometimes use brush strips held in plastic carriers for doors, as well as the more common brushes used across the bottoms of doors. Letterplate brushes and ones with flaps in white and brown are used too, as are brush pile self-adhesive strips in brown, white and grey and universal replacement rubber seals for uPVC windows.

We use both white decorator's caulk and various types of silicone (white, clear, brown and black), which are best not used against painted surfaces except outside.

Heat Loss Checklist

Here is a checklist of things that are trying to cool your home during the winter. You should go through this list to assess which ones are causing problems in your home, and then take remedial action to mitigate the impacts. They are not in any kind of priority order, as every house is different, and the extent to which each problem will be happening in each house is also different. Although it's impossible to prioritise them, I have put nearer the top the ones that I see as having a greater impact.

- Cavity walls
- Dot-and-dabbed walls
- Ventilated underfloor voids
- Heated conservatories
- Party walls
- Extractor fans
- Trickle vents
- First-floor voids
- Dormer bungalow first-floor voids
- Letterboxes and letterplate flaps
- Sliding sash windows
- Gaps under window and door sills
- Open flues
- Redundant combustion air bricks
- Soil and vent pipe casings
- Ventilated chimneys
- Thermal bypass in a warm roof at gable and eaves roof-wall junctions
- Dormer windows
- Steel-framed windows
- Cat flaps
- Draughty roof windows – check draught seals on closing bar
- Cold-water cisterns (toilets and cold water tank) – importing cold water that gets warmed up by the house interior before being flushed away warm
- Drying clothes indoors – latent heat of evaporation is sucked out of the house interior
- Drying logs indoors – as above
- Bringing anything cold into the house
- Lintels
- Loft hatch
- Opening windows every morning to get rid of the condensation
- Radiators on external walls
- Curtains that drape over radiators
- Open plan and missing internal doors and/or overly high ceilings
- Overflow pipes
- Balconies, cantilevers and so on that bridge insulation
- Single-glazed windows
- Badly fitted floorboards and door frames

History of Reading DraughtBusters

DraughtBusters applied for funding from Reading Borough Council and were awarded a grant via Transition Town Reading Energy Group in late 2012 to buy the materials for a draught-busting project. That was the start of DraughtBusters. Since then, Draught-Busters has built up a team of experienced volunteers who have helped a lot of people living in energy poverty and in cold and draughty homes. These people have also been given advice on ventilation, as well as on how to manage their heating systems.

DraughtBusters continues to provide practical help to people struggling to pay their heating bills. You can read more about who we help below, but most, if not all, homes could benefit from some additional draughtproofing, and it is not hard to do. The average cost per home for the materials used by DraughtBusters was initially just £22 (we buy in bulk). This rose to £25 by the end of 2017 and to £28 during 2022.

The draughtproofing service targets those in most need; the priority groups are those living in energy poverty, families with young children, the elderly, vulnerable and people under debt management. We have also helped others when they ask. Many clients are referred to DraughtBusters through Citizens Advice, the council's Winter Watch scheme, the hospital, local debt advice agencies, GPs, churches and charities. Others contact us directly, often because they've been told about us by someone who has previously been helped by the DraughtBusters scheme. Initially, about a third of our clients used to come through those types of recommendations; lately, more are coming to us direct through our website.

During the autumn of 2021, I was approached by a group in a nearby town who wanted to set up a DraughtBusters project of their own. I did a talk, a seminar and a workshop for them, gave them a basic pack of draughtproofing materials and helped them with their first two DraughtBusts, since which time they have been very successfully flying solo. Over the following six months, a further seven local towns have started the process of initiating DraughtBusters groups, as well as one on the Isle of Wight, with which I helped remotely.

The DraughtBusters website (readinguk.org/draughtbusters/) has been developed as a way of sharing some of the things that we have learnt from the work carried out in houses in and around Reading. This information is provided in the hope that others in similar situations will be able to do their own draughtproofing.